BIRDS, BEASTS
AND FLOWERS

Birds, Beasts

 A BLACK SPARROW BOOK
DAVID R. GODINE ·Publisher· Boston

POEMS BY

D. H. LAWRENCE

INTRODUCTION BY

KEITH CUSHMAN

and Flowers

This is a Black Sparrow Book
published in 2007 by
DAVID R. GODINE · *Publisher*
Post Office Box 450
Jaffrey, New Hampshire 03452
www.blacksparrowbooks.com

BIRDS, BEASTS AND FLOWERS

From COLLECTED POEMS by D. H. Lawrence. Copyright © Jonathan Cape and
Harrison Smith, Inc., 1929. Copyright renewed Frieda Lawrence Ravagli, 1957.
Reprinted by arrangement with Viking Penguin, a division of Penguin Books USA Inc.
Introduction copyright © 2007 by Keith Cushman
The cover reproduces D. H. Lawrence's design for the dust jacket of the first edition
of BIRDS, BEASTS AND FLOWERS. (Thomas Seltzer, 1923) This book reprints the
first edition with a few corrections of typographical errors and the restoration of
a number of lines considered indecent in 1923.

LIBRARY OF CONGRESS CATALOGING-IN-PUBLICATION DATA
Lawrence, D. H. (David Herbert), 1885–1930.
Birds, beasts and flowers/D.H. Lawrence.
p.   cm.
ISBN-10 0-87685-866-3 (paperback)
ISBN-13978-0-87685-866-0
I. Title. II. Title: Birds, beasts, and flowers.
PR6023.A93B5   1992
821'.912—dc20
92701 CIP

FIFTH PRINTING
Printed in Canada

CONTENTS

BIRDS, BEASTS AND FLOWERS

I. LAWRENCE THE POET

In *D. H. Lawrence: A Personal Record* (1935) Jessie Chambers, the woman who was the prototype of Miriam in Lawrence's autobiographical novel *Sons and Lovers*, tells how she first learned of the young Lawrence's ambition to become a poet. One night Lawrence "with eyes alight" announced:

> "It will be *poetry*."
> I took fire at that.
> "Well, isn't that the very greatest thing?"
> "Ah, you say that," he replied. "But what will the others say?
> That I'm a fool. A collier's son a poet!"

D. H. Lawrence (1885–1930) traveled far from his origins as a coal-miner's son to become one of the twentieth century's greatest English novelists. His masterpieces are *Sons and Lovers* (1913), *The Rainbow* (1915), *Women in Love* (1920), and the enduringly notorious *Lady Chatterley's Lover* (1928). Lawrence was an accomplished, prolific writer in many genres. During his short lifetime he published six other novels (plus a novel he collaborated on with an Australian nurse), seven novellas, about seventy-five short stories, eight plays, four travel books, two books of home-made psychological theory, much literary criticism including a ground-breaking study of classic American literature, much miscellaneous prose, and a school history textbook—while also writing amost six thousand letters. Ultimately that collier's son also became one of the most important English-language poets of the twentieth century.

INTRODUCTION

Lawrence wrote poetry throughout his career: *Love Poems and Others* (1913) was his third book, and the posthumous *Last Poems* (1932) was one of his finest collections. *The Complete Poems*, the best available edition of Lawrence's poetry, runs to almost 1100 pages, including some juvenilia and variant drafts. The forthcoming authoritative Cambridge University Press edition of the poetry will fill three volumes.

Lawrence's poetry stands in opposition to the poetry of such great twentieth-century formalists as William Butler Yeats, T. S. Eliot, and Wallace Stevens. Lawrence began his career working within the constraints of traditional poetic form: meter, rhyme, and stanza. Often he found this form confining. In many early poems the form seems to be manipulating the poet rather than the reverse. Even as a young poet he defined his poetry against the conventional poetry of his era, which he saw as "scraps sweetly moulded in easy Plaster of Paris sentiment." Authenticity and emotional integrity came first to Lawrence. He liked "sincerity, and a quickening spontaneous emotion," and—significantly —his poems had "some blood in them." In Lawrence's most important exposition of his poetic beliefs, the essay called "Poetry of the Present" (1918), he distinguishes between poems of "exquisite finality, perfection" whose "completeness" and "consummateness . . . are conveyed in exquisite form" and *his* kind of poetry, which he calls "poetry of the present." The very perfection of the "treasured gem-like lyrics of Shelley and Keats" means that these poems leave out the "inconclusiveness" and "immediacy" of "life itself."

II. Birds, Beasts and Flowers

Birds, Beasts and Flowers (1923), universally regarded as Lawrence's finest volume of poetry, is one of the most notable English-language poetry monographs of the first half of the twentieth century. Lawrence expressed his own sense of accomplishment when he sent the manuscript to Thomas Seltzer, his American publisher: "I feel rather strongly about this book of verse: feel it is really my best."

Lawrence took his title from the second verse of the sweetly senti-mental Victorian hymn, "Now the day is over":

Now the darkness gathers,
Stars begin to peep,
Birds, and beasts and flowers
Soon will be asleep.

The title resonates ironically, for Lawrence's poems are anything but Christian.

The poems of *Birds, Beasts* evoke and reflect on the "birds, beasts, and flowers" Lawrence encountered during his travels between 1919 and 1923. He and his wife Frieda left England for Italy in November 1919, a year after the Armistice that ended World War I. On 30 November 1920 he reported to the American poet Amy Lowell from Sicily that he had completed "a little book of *vers libre* [free verse]—*Birds, Beasts and Flowers.*" Only Italian flora and fauna figured in this earli-est conception of the book. By the time *Birds, Beasts* was published almost three years later in October 1923 it had grown substantially. It had also taken on some characteristics of a travelogue with a number of poems set in the American Southwest and two poems marking way-stations in the Lawrences' journey from Italy to Taos, New Mexico. "Elephant" is the product of the six weeks the Lawrences spent visit-ing American friends in Ceylon (now Sri Lanka), while "Kangaroo" grew out of their six-week stay in Australia.

Birds, Beasts and Flowers is a collection of unusual "nature poems." One of the impressive qualities of the poems is their immediacy and seeming spontaneity. Lawrence has abandoned traditional poetic form altogether in these mostly lengthy poems. Instead, the poems' long, sinuous, unrhymed lines reveal the unmistakable influence of Walt Whitman's *Leaves of Grass.* In "Poetry of the Present" Lawrence declares that poetry of the living present should aim to capture the "quivering momentaneity" of life. He adds that "Whitman's is the best poetry of this kind."

INTRODUCTION

The *Birds, Beasts* poems attempt to express the elemental energy and "otherness" of a pomegranate, fig-trees, purple anemones, a mosquito, a fish, or whatever the poet is encountering. The poems are not exactly descriptive. Instead, as the critic Graham Hough explained half-a-century ago, Lawrence "makes an energetic and intuitive attempt to penetrate into the being of natural objects, to show what they are in themselves, not how they can sustain our moral nature."

But *Birds, Beasts and Flowers* is more than a collection of Lawrentian nature poems. As with the novels *Aaron's Rod* (1922) and *Kangaroo* (1923) that date from this period, the *Birds, Beasts* poems provided Lawrence with an avenue for developing his ideas. For example, in "Kangaroo" the animal's eyes that have "watched so many empty dawns in silent Australia" point to Lawrence's perception of something prehistoric about the female kangaroo. He observes all the animal's "weight, all her blood, dripping sack-wise down towards the earth's centre." As the poem concludes he urges the kangaroo to leap "and come down on the line that draws to the earth's deep, heavy centre." The kangaroo, somehow the vestige of an earlier, pre-civilized world, is connected to darkly sustaining energies that have been lost to modern humanity. Thus "Kangaroo" is at once an attempt to express the inner reality of the animal and a meditation on the purer world that predated civilization.

"Pomegranate," "Peach," and "Medlars and Sorb-Apples" ("I love you, rotten, / Delicious rottenness") dramatize Lawrence's embrace of organic life, including decay and death, and his attack on a society that prefers the security of something "round and finished like a billiard ball" to the "blood-red, deep" peach. "Bare Fig Trees" turns into a criticism of democracy. The four "Evangelistic Beasts" poems attack Christian idealism. For example, the powerful, intensely sexual bull of St. Luke has been "bewitched" by the "Son of Man" and is left "moaning, booing, roaring" in frustration.

One of the secrets of *Birds, Beasts and Flowers* is that the poems refuse to allegorize the creatures and plants—but at the same time to some extent they do allegorize them. This mixed, seemingly inconsistent mode is not a failing. Indeed it is crucial to the originality and accomplishment of the poems and part of the reason that they are so lively, provocative, and intellectually stimulating. The poems fail only when the balance tips toward polemic, as in "The Evening Land" and "The American Eagle," two anti-American screeds. "Fig," the most notorious poem in the collection, swiftly reveals itself as an attack on modern female sexuality.

Over the years critics have attempted to read *Birds, Beasts and Flowers* as a systematic exposition (or at least exploration) of Lawrence's "philosophy" in this period. In my opinion no one has successfully located any such system. Certainly the poems are all of a piece in their poise, brio, and confidence, as well as in their subject matter. Certainly the ideas expressed in the poems are almost always engaging. But the attentive reader will respond differently to different poems. "Peach" and "Mosquito" are notable for their wit. "Elephant" brings to life a night-time ritual procession in Ceylon with brilliant poetic immediacy. "Mountain Lion" is a haunting evocation of modern civilization's violation and destruction of the natural world. "The Revolutionary" (in which Lawrence imagines himself as the blind Samson longing to bring down the "pillars that hold up the dome of high ideal heaven"), "The Red Wolf," and "Spirits Summoned West" are all movingly personal. The *Birds, Beasts and Flowers* poems are all of a piece and yet surprisingly various.

III. "Snake"

"Snake," the best-known and most-anthologized of Lawrence's poems, recounts and dramatizes an experience Lawrence may have had while living in Taormina, Sicily, in July 1920. The finest, most famous poem in *Birds, Beasts and Flowers* deserves some brief commentary.

Lawrence's snake is something of a mythic figure. It is a "king in exile, uncrowned in the underworld, / Now due to be crowned again." At the same time Lawrence finds the words (many of which begin with a snake-like sibilant "s") to express the snake-ness of the snake.

"Snake" stages the conflict between the two sides of the poet's nature. He spontaneously *likes* the snake and is pleased to welcome it to his water-trough. But the "voice of [his] education" warns him that the snake "must be killed, / For in Sicily the black, black snakes are innocent, the gold are venomous." His "accursed human education" tells him that "If [he] were a man," "[he] would take a stick and break him now, and finish him off." When the snake puts "his head into that dreadful hole, . . . snake-easing his shoulders, and enter[s] further, / A sort of horror, a sort of protest against his withdrawing into that horrid black hole, . . . Overcame me now his back was turned." The poet's "education" wins out: he throws a log at the snake, which "Writhe[s] like lightning" and disappears "Into the black hole." At the end of the poem the poet is thinking about Coleridge's albatross. He is left with "something to expiate: / A pettiness."

"Snake" brilliantly dramatizes Lawrence's ideas about the otherness of the natural world and civilization's fear of the darkness—both inner and outer—concealed beneath the surface of life. The poem's imagery makes it clear that human sexuality is one aspect of the threatening darkness. The poet realizes that in the end he has "missed [his] chance with one of the lords / Of life."

IV. The prefatory notes and the dust jacket design

The rather cryptic notes—Lawrence called them "hundred-word captions" and "bits"—that preface nine sections of *Birds, Beasts and Flowers* did not appear in the American or English first editions of the book, both published in 1923. Lawrence wrote them in the summer of 1929 for a deluxe edition of the book with wood-engravings by Blair Hughes-Stanton, published by the Cresset Press in June 1930. The quotations are partly drawn from fragments of early Greek philosophy and partly original. Lawrence had been dead three months by the time the Cresset Press *Birds, Beasts and Flowers* was published.

Lawrence himself designed the dust jacket of *Birds, Beasts and Flowers*. The design is at once energetic, playful, and marvelously balanced. In the relationship between title and iconic figures, in lettering style, and in overall design the jacket is reminiscent of the title pages of some of William Blake's prophetic books. As the work of the poet, the jacket design of *Birds, Beasts and Flowers* has special interpretive authority.

The exuberant exclamation point after *Flowers*, which appears nowhere else on or in the book, emphasizes the mood of many of the poems. The fruits in the panel directly below the title are appropriately sexualized—with a comic touch: the split-open pomegranate in the center seems to reveal somebody's chubby rear end and legs. The oddly upright phallus-shaped fish against a background of Southwestern pines on the left is balanced on the right by a naked woman whom I take to be Eve (complete with cleft) beside a tree that evokes the Tree of the Knowledge of Good and Evil. Humanity's fall from innocence into self-consciousness is a theme in many of the poems. The male–female polarity of these two figures points to an important motif in the book (though it must be said that the phallic fish seems to display a split of its own).

The dog on the left seems to be an English bulldog. The bull on the right is an evangelistic beast, the emblem of St. Luke. Lawrence has paired these two animals for the sake of a sort of visual pun: bulldog/bull.

The boldly stylized eagle grasping a snake (with its tongue sticking out) at the top of the jacket is the most striking design element. This is not the American eagle of the shrill poem that concludes the collection nor is it the snake that came to Lawrence's water-trough in Taormina, Sicily. Instead, the image of eagle with snake in its talons is the central icon of Mexican post-colonial identity. I believe that this image, which has no real connection with *Birds, Beasts and Flowers*, is a more personal reference. Lawrence and Frieda were in Mexico City from 24 March to 27 April 1923. The eagle/snake image seems to celebrate his first visit to Mexico—the setting of his next novel, *The Plumed Serpent*.

INTRODUCTION

One of the early reviews of *Birds, Beasts and Flowers* praised D. H. Lawrence as a "subtly creative artist of vision who makes us see things with his fine and deep perceptions." That statement remains true eighty-five years later, and the poems of *Birds, Beasts and Flowers* are as fresh and enjoyable as ever.

KEITH CUSHMAN
University of North Carolina at Greensboro

FRUITS

"For fruits are all of them female, in them lies the seed. And so when they break and show the seed, then we look into the womb and see its secrets. So it is that the pomegranate is the apple of love to the Arab, and the

fig has been a catch-word for the female fissure for ages. I don't care a fig for it! men say. But why a fig? The apple of Eden, even, was Eve's fruit. To her it belonged, and she offered it to the man. Even the apples of knowledge are Eve's fruit, the woman's. But the apples of life the dragon guards, and no woman gives them. . . ."

"No sin is it to drink as much as a man can take and get home without a servant's help, so he be not stricken in years."

Pomegranate

You tell me I am wrong.
Who are you, who is anybody to tell me I am wrong?
I am not wrong.

In Syracuse, rock left bare by the viciousness of Greek women,
No doubt you have forgotten the pomegranate trees in flower,
Oh so red, and such a lot of them.

Whereas at Venice
Abhorrent, green, slippery city
Whose Doges were old, and had ancient eyes,
In the dense foliage of the inner garden
Pomegranates like bright green stone,
And barbed, barbed with a crown.
Oh, crown of spiked green metal
Actually growing!

Now, in Tuscany,
Pomegranates to warm your hands at;
And crowns, kingly, generous, tilting crowns
Over the left eyebrow.

And, if you dare, the fissure!

Do you mean to tell me you will see no fissure?
Do you prefer to look on the plain side?

For all that, the setting suns are open.
The end cracks open with the beginning:
Rosy, tender, glittering within the fissure.

FRUITS

Do you mean to tell me there should be no fissure?
No glittering, compact drops of dawn?
Do you mean it is wrong, the gold-filmed skin, integument,
     shown ruptured?

For my part, I prefer my heart to be broken.
It is so lovely, dawn-kaleidoscopic within the crack.

San Gervasio in Tuscany

Peach

Would you like to throw a stone at me?
Here, take all that's left of my peach.

Blood-red, deep;
Heaven knows how it came to pass.
Somebody's pound of flesh rendered up.

Wrinkled with secrets
And hard with the intention to keep them.

Why, from silvery peach-bloom,
From that shallow-silvery wine-glass on a short stem
This rolling, dropping, heavy globule?

I am thinking, of course, of the peach before I ate it.

Why so velvety, why so voluptuous heavy?
Why hanging with such inordinate weight?
Why so indented?

Why the groove?
Why the lovely, bivalve roundnesses?
Why the ripple down the sphere?
Why the suggestion of incision?

Why was not my peach round and finished like a billiard ball?
It would have been if man had made it.
Though I've eaten it now.

FRUITS

But it wasn't round and finished like a billiard ball;
And because I say so, you would like to throw something at me.
Here, you can have my peach stone.

San Gervasio

Fig

The proper way to eat a fig, in society,
Is to split it in four, holding it by the stump,
And open it, so that it is a glittering, rosy, moist, honied,
       heavy-petalled four-petalled flower.

Then you throw away the skin
Which is just like a four-sepalled calyx,
After you have taken off the blossom with your lips.

But the vulgar way
Is just to put your mouth to the crack, and take out the flesh
       in one bite.

Every fruit has its secret.

The fig is a very secretive fruit.
As you see it standing growing, you feel at once it is symbolic:
And it seems male.
But when you come to know it better, you agree with the Romans,
       it is female.

The Italians vulgarly say, it stands for the female part; the fig-fruit:
The fissure, the yoni,
The wonderful moist conductivity towards the centre.

Involved,
Inturned,
The flowering all inward and womb-fibrilled;
And but one orifice.

The fig, the horse-shoe, the squash blossom.
Symbols.

FRUITS

There was a flower that flowered inward, womb-ward;
Now there is a fruit like a ripe womb.

It was always a secret.
That's how it should be, always be secret.

There never was any standing aloft and unfolded on a bough
Like other flowers, in a revelation of petals;
Silver-pink peach, venetian green glass of medlars and sorb-apples,
Shallow wine-cups on short, bulging stems
Openly pledging heaven:
Here's to the thorn in flower! Here is to Utterance!
The brave, adventurous rosaceae.

Folded upon itself, and secret unutterable,
And milky-sapped, sap that curdles milk and makes *ricotta*,
Sap that smells strange on your fingers, that even goats won't taste it;
Folded upon itself, enclosed like any Mohammedan woman,
Its nakedness all within-walls, its flowering forever unseen,
One small way of access only, and this close-curtained from the light;
Fig, fruit of the female mystery, covert and inward,
Mediterranean fruit, with your covert nakedness,
Where everything happens invisible, flowering and fertilisation,
        and fruiting
In the inwardness of your You, that eye will never see
Till it's finished, and you're over-ripe, and you burst to give up
        your ghost.

Till the drop of ripeness exudes,
And the year is over.

And then the fig has kept her secret long enough.
So it explodes, and you see through the fissure the scarlet.
And the fig is finished, the year is over.

8

That's how the fig dies, showing her crimson through the purple slit
Like a wound, the exposure of her secret, on the open day.
Like a prostitute, the bursten fig, making a show of her secret.

That's how women die too.

The year is fallen over-ripe,
The year of our women.
The year of our women is fallen over-ripe.
The secret is laid bare.
The year of our women is fallen over-ripe.

When Eve once knew *in her mind* that she was naked
She quickly sewed fig-leaves, and sewed the same for the man.
She'd been naked all her days before,
But till then, till that apple of knowledge, she hadn't thought about it.

She got the fact on her mind, and quickly sewed fig-leaves.
And women have been sewing ever since.
But now they stitch to adorn the bursten fig, not to cover it.
They have their nakedness more than ever on their mind,
And they won't let us forget it.

Now, the secret
Becomes an affirmation through moist, scarlet lips
That laugh at the Lord's indignation.

What then, good Lord! cry the women.
We have kept our secret long enough.
We are a ripe fig.
Let us burst into affirmation.

They forget, ripe figs won't keep.
Ripe figs won't keep.

FRUITS

Honey-white figs of the North, black figs with scarlet inside,
    of the South.
Ripe figs won't keep, won't keep in any clime.
What then, when women the world over have all bursten
    into affirmation?
And bursten figs won't keep?

San Gervasio

Medlars and Sorb-Apples

I love you, rotten,
Delicious rottenness.

I love to suck you out from your skins
So brown and soft and coming suave,
So morbid, as the Italians say.

What a rare, powerful, reminiscent flavour
Comes out of your falling through the stages of decay:
Stream within stream.

Something of the same flavour as Syracusan muscat wine
Or vulgar Marsala.

Though even the word Marsala will smack of preciosity
Soon in the pussy-foot West.

What is it?
What is it, in the grape turning raisin,
In the medlar, in the sorb-apple,
Wineskins of brown morbidity,
Autumnal excrementa;
What is it that reminds us of white gods?

Gods nude as blanched nut-kernels,
Strangely, half sinisterly flesh-fragrant
As if with sweat,
And drenched with mystery.

Sorb-apples, medlars with dead crowns.
I say, wonderful are the hellish experiences,

FRUITS

Orphic, delicate
Dionysos of the Underworld.

A kiss, and a spasm of farewell, a moment's orgasm of rupture,
Then along the damp road alone, till the next turning.
And there, a new partner, a new parting, a new unfusing into twain,
A new gasp of further isolation,
A new intoxication of loneliness, among decaying, frost-cold leaves.

Going down the strange lanes of hell, more and more intensely alone,
The fibres of the heart parting one after the other
And yet the soul continuing, naked-footed, ever more vividly embodied
Like a flame blown whiter and whiter
In a deeper and deeper darkness
Ever more exquisite, distilled in separation.

So, in the strange retorts of medlars and sorb-apples
The distilled essence of hell.
The exquisite odour of leave-taking. *Jamque vale!*
Orpheus, and the winding, leaf-clogged, silent lanes of hell.

Each soul departing with its own isolation,
Strangest of all strange companions,
And best.

Medlars, sorb-apples
More than sweet
Flux of autumn
Sucked out of your empty bladders
And sipped down, perhaps, with a sip of Marsala
So that the rambling, sky-dropped grape can add its music to yours,

Orphic farewell, and farewell, and farewell
And the *ego sum* of Dionysos
The *sono io* of perfect drunkenness
Intoxication of final loneliness.

San Gervasio

Grapes

So many fruits come from roses
From the rose of all roses
From the unfolded rose
Rose of all the world.

Admit that apples and strawberries and peaches and pears
        and blackberries
Are all Rosaceae,
Issue of the explicit rose,
The open-countenanced, skyward-smiling rose.

What then of the vine?
Oh, what of the tendrilled vine?

Ours is the universe of the unfolded rose,
The explicit
The candid revelation.

But long ago, oh, long ago
Before the rose began to smile supreme,
Before the rose of all roses, rose of all the world, was even in bud,
Before the glaciers were gathered up in a bunch out of the unsettled
        seas and winds,
Or else before they had been let down again, in Noah's flood,
There was another world, a dusky, flowerless, tendrilled world
And creatures webbed and marshy,
And on the margin, men soft-footed and pristine
Still, and sensitive, and active,
Audile, tactile sensitiveness as of a tendril which orientates and
        reaches out,
Reaching out and grasping by an instinct more delicate than
        the moon's as she feels for the tides.

Of which world, the vine was the invisible rose,
Before petals spread, before colour made its disturbance, before
    eyes saw too much.
In a green, muddy, web-foot, utterly songless world
The vine was rose of all roses.
There were no poppies or carnations,
Hardly a greenish lily, watery faint.
Green, dim, invisible flourishing of vines
Royally gesticulate.

Look now, even now, how it keeps its power of invisibility!
Look how black, how blue-black, how gloved in Ethiopian darkness
Dropping among his leaves, hangs the dark grape!
See him there, the swart, so palpably invisible!
Whom shall we ask about him?
The negro might know a little.
When the vine was rose, Gods were dark-skinned.
Bacchus is a dream's dream.
Once God was all negroid, as now he is fair.
But it is so long ago, the ancient Bushman has forgotten more utterly
    than we, who have never known.

Yet we are on the brink of re-remembrance.
Which, I suppose, is why America has gone dry.
Our pale day is sinking into twilight,
And if we sip the wine, we find dreams coming upon us
Out of the imminent night.
Nay, we find ourselves crossing the fern-scented frontiers
Of the world before the floods, where man was dark and evasive
And the tiny vine-flower rose of all roses, perfumed,
And all in naked communion communicating as now our clothed
    vision can never communicate.
Vistas, down dark avenues
As we sip the wine.

FRUITS

The grape is swart, the avenues dusky and tendrilled, subtly prehensile,
But we, as we start awake, clutch at our vistas democratic, boulevards,
      tram-cars, policemen.
Give us our own back
Let us go to the soda-fountain, to get sober.

Soberness, sobriety.
It is like the agonised perverseness of a child heavy with sleep,
      yet fighting, fighting to keep awake;
Soberness, sobriety, with heavy eyes propped open.

Dusky are the avenues of wine,
And we must cross the frontiers, though we will not,
Of the lost, fern-scented world:
Take the fern-seed on our lips
Close the eyes, and go
Down the tendrilled avenues of wine and the otherworld.

San Gervasio

THE REVOLUTIONARY

Look at them standing there in authority
The pale-faces,
As if it could have effect any more.

Pale-face authority,
Caryatids,
Pillars of white bronze standing rigid, lest the skies fall.

What a job they've got to keep it up.
Their poor, idealist foreheads naked capitals
To the entablature of clouded heaven.

When the skies are going to fall, fall they will
In a great chute and rush of débâcle downwards.

Oh, and I wish the high and super-gothic heavens would come
        down now,
The heavens above, that we yearn to and aspire to.

I do not yearn, nor aspire, for I am a blind Samson.
And what is daylight to me that I should look skyward?
Only I grope among you, pale-faces, caryatids, as among a forest
        of pillars that hold up the dome of high ideal heaven
Which is my prison,
And all these human pillars of loftiness, going stiff, metallic-stunned
        with the weight of their responsibility
I stumble against them.
Stumbling-blocks, painful ones.

To keep on holding up this ideal civilisation
Must be excruciating: unless you stiffen into metal, when it is easier
        to stand stock rigid than to move.

THE REVOLUTIONARY

This is why I tug at them, individually, with my arm round their waist
The human pillars.
They are not stronger than I am, blind Samson.
The house sways.

I shall be so glad when it comes down.
I am so tired of the limitations of their Infinite.
I am so sick of the pretensions of the Spirit.
I am so weary of pale-face importance.

Am I not blind, at the round-turning mill?
Then why should I fear their pale faces?
Or love the effulgence of their switched-on holy light?
The glare of their righteousness?

To me, all faces are dark,
All lips are dusky and valved.

Save your lips, oh pale-faces!
Which are slips of metal,
Slits in an automatic-machine, you columns of give-and-take.

To me, the earth rolls ponderously, superbly
Coming my way without forethought or afterthought.
To me, men's footfalls fall with a dull, soft rumble, ominous and lovely,
Coming my way.

But not your foot-falls, pale-faces!
They are a clicketing of bits and disjointed metal
Working in motion.

To me, men are palpable, invisible nearnesses in the dark
Sending out magnetic vibrations of warning, pitch-dark throbs
        of invitation.

THE REVOLUTIONARY

But you, pale-faces,
You are painful, harsh-surfaced pillars that give off nothing
     except rigidity,
And I jut against you if I try to move, for you are everywhere,
     and I am blind,
Sightless among all your visuality,
You staring Caryatids.

See if I don't bring you down, and all your high opinion
And all your ponderous roofed-in erection of right and wrong,
Your particular heavens,
With a smash.

See if your skies aren't falling!
And my head, at least, is thick enough to stand it, the smash.

See if I don't move under a dark and nude, vast heaven
When your world is in ruins, under your fallen skies.
Caryatids, pale-faces.
See if I am not Lord of the dark and moving hosts
Before I die.

Florence

THE EVENING LAND

Oh America
The sun sets in you.
Are you the grave of our day?

Shall I come to you, the open tomb of my race?

I would come, if I felt my hour had struck.
I would rather you came to me.

For that matter
Mahomet never went to any mountain
Save it had first approached him and cajoled his soul.

You have cajoled the souls of millions of us
America,
Why won't you cajole my soul?
I wish you would.

I confess I am afraid of you.

The catastrophe of your exaggerate love,
You who never find yourself, in love,
But only lose yourself further, decomposing.

You who never recover from out of the orgasm of loving
Your pristine, isolate integrity, lost aeons ago.
Your singleness within the universe.

You who in loving break down
And break further and further down
Your bounds of isolation,

But who never rise, resurrected, from this grave of mingling,
In a new proud singleness, America.

Your more-than-European idealism,
Like a be-aureoled bleached skeleton hovering
Its cage-ribs in the social heaven, beneficent.

And then your rapid resurrection
Into machine-uprisen perfect man.

Even the winged skeleton of your bleached ideal
Is not so frightening as that clean smooth
Automaton of your uprisen self,
Machine America.

Do you wonder that I am afraid to come
And answer the first machine-cut question from the lips of
        your useful men?
Put the first cents into hinged fingers of your officers
And sit beside the steel-straight arms of your fair women,
American?

This may be a withering tree, this Europe,
But here, even a customs-official is still vulnerable.

I am so terrified, America,
Of the iron click of your human contact.
And after this
The winding-sheet of your self-less ideal love.
Boundless love
Like a poison gas.

Does no one realise that love should be particular, individual,
Not boundless.

THE EVENING LAND

This boundless love is like the bad smell
Of something gone wrong in the middle.
All of this philanthropy and benevolence on other people's behalf
Just a bad smell.

Yet, America, sometimes
Your elvishness, elves wanton, elves wistful;
Your New England uncanniness,
Your western brutal faery quality.

My soul is half-cajoled, half-cajoled.

Something in you which carries me beyond
Yankee, Yankee,
What we call human.
Carries me where I want to be carried . . .

Or don't I?

What does it matter
What we call human, and what we don't call human?
The rose would smell as sweet.
And to be limited by a mere word is to be less than a hopping flea,
      which hops over such an obstruction at first jump.

Your horrible, skeleton, aureoled ideal,
Your weird bright motor-productive mechanism,
Two spectres.

But moreoever
A dark, unfathomed will, that is not unJewish;
A set, stoic endurance, non-European;
An ultimate desperateness, unAfrican;
A deliberate generosity, non-Oriental.

THE EVENING LAND

The strange, unaccustomed geste of your demonish New World nature
Glimpsed now and then.

Nobody knows you.
You don't know yourself.
And I, who am half in love with you,
What am I in love with?
My own imaginings?

Say it is not so.
Say, through the branches
America, America
Of all your machines,
Say, in the deep sockets of your idealistic skull,
Dark, aboriginal eyes
Stoic, able to wait through ages
Glancing.

Say, in the sound of all your machines
And white words, white-washed American,
Deep pulsing of a strange heart
New throb, like a stirring under the false dawn that precedes the real.

Nascent American
Demonish, lurking among the undergrowth
Of many-stemmed machines and chimneys that smoke like pine trees.

Dark, elvish,
Modern, unissued, uncanny America,
Your nascent demon people
Lurking among the deeps of your industrial thicket
Allure me till I am beside myself,
A nympholept.

"These States!" as Whitman said,
Whatever he meant.   *Baden-Baden*

PEACE

Peace is written on the doorstep
In lava.

Peace, black peace congealed.
My heart will know no peace
Till the hill bursts.

Brilliant, intolerable lava
Brilliant as a powerful burning-glass
Walking like a royal snake down the mountain towards the sea.

Forests, cities, bridges
Gone again in the bright trail of lava.
Naxos thousands of feet below the olive-roots,
And now the olive leaves thousands of feet below the lava fire.

Peace congealed in black lava on the doorstep.
Within, white-hot lava, never at peace
Till it burst forth blinding, withering the earth;
To set again into rock
Grey-black rock.

Call it Peace?

Taormina

TREES

"It is said, a disease has attacked the cypress trees of Italy, and they are all dying.
Now even the shadow of the lost secret is vanishing from earth."
"Empedokles says trees were the first living creatures to grow up out of the earth, before the sun was spread out and before day and night were distinguished; from the symmetry of their mixture of fire and water, they contain the proportion of male and female; they grow, rising up owing to the heat which is in the earth, so that they are parts of the earth just as embryos are parts of the uterus. Fruits are excretions of the water and fire in plants."

Cypresses

Tuscan cypresses,
What is it?

Folded in like a dark thought
For which the language is lost,
Tuscan cypresses,
Is there a great secret?
Are our words no good?

The undeliverable secret,
Dead with a dead race and a dead speech, and yet
Darkly monumental in you,
Etruscan cypresses.

Ah, how I admire your fidelity,
Dark cypresses.

Is it the secret of the long-nosed Etruscans?
The long-nosed, sensitive-footed, subtly-smiling Etruscans,
Who made so little noise outside the cypress groves?

Among the sinuous, flame-tall cypresses
That swayed their length of darkness all around
Etruscan-dusky, wavering men of old Etruria:
Naked except for fanciful long shoes,
Going with insidious, half-smiling quietness
And some of Africa's imperturbable sang-froid
About a forgotten business.

What business, then?
Nay, tongues are dead, and words are hollow as hollow seed-pods,
Having shed their sound and finished all their echoing

TREES

Etruscan syllables,
That had the telling.

Yet more I see you darkly concentrate,
Tuscan cypresses,
On one old thought:
On one old slim imperishable thought, while you remain
Etruscan cypresses;
Dusky, slim marrow-thought of slender, flickering men of Etruria,
Whom Rome called vicious.

Vicious, dark cypresses:
Vicious, you supple, brooding, softly-swaying pillars of dark flame.
Monumental to a dead, dead race
Embowered in you!

Were they then vicious, the slender, tender-footed
Long-nosed men of Etruria?
Or was their way only evasive and different, dark, like cypress-trees
    in a wind?

They are dead, with all their vices,
And all that is left
Is the shadowy monomania of some cypresses
And tombs.

The smile, the subtle Etruscan smile still lurking
Within the tombs,
Etruscan cypresses.

He laughs longest who laughs last;
Nay, Leonardo only bungled the pure Etruscan smile.

What would I not give
To bring back the rare and orchid-like
Evil-yclept Etruscan?
For as to the evil
We have only Roman word for it,
Which I, being a little weary of Roman virtue,
Don't hang much weight on.

For oh, I know, in the dust where we have buried
The silenced races and all their abominations,
We have buried so much of the delicate magic of life.

There in the deeps
That churn the frankincense and ooze the myrrh,
Cypress shadowy,
Such an aroma of lost human life!

They say the fit survive,
But I invoke the spirits of the lost.
Those that have not survived, the darkly lost,
To bring their meaning back into life again,
Which they have taken away
And wrapt inviolable in soft cypress trees,
Etruscan cypresses.

Evil, what is evil?
There is only one evil, to deny life
As Rome denied Etruria
And mechanical America Montezuma still.

Fiesole

Bare Fig-Trees

Fig-trees, weird fig-trees
Made of thick smooth silver,
Made of sweet, untarnished silver in the sea-southern air—
I say untarnished, but I mean opaque—
Thick, smooth-fleshed silver, dull only as human limbs are dull
With the life-lustre,
Nude with the dim light of full, healthy life
That is always half-dark,
And suave like passion-flower petals,
Like passion-flowers,
With the half-secret gleam of a passion-flower hanging from the rock,
Great, complicated, nude fig-tree, stemless flower-mesh.
Flowerily naked in flesh, and giving off hues of life;
Rather like an octopus, but strange and sweet-myriad-limbed octopus;
Like a nude, like a rock-living, sweet-fleshed sea-anemone
Flourishing from the rock in a mysterious arrogance.

Let me sit down beneath the many-branching candelabrum
That lives upon this rock
And laugh at Time, and laugh at dull Eternity
And make a joke of stale Infinity
Within the flesh-scent of this wicked tree
That has kept so many secrets up its sleeve
And has been laughing through so many ages
At man and his uncomfortablenesses,
And his attempt to assure himself that what is so is not so,
Up its sleeve.

Let me sit down beneath this many-branching candelabrum,
The Jewish seven-branched, holy-stinking candlestick kicked
        over the cliff

And all its stiff-necked righteousness got rid of,
And let me notice it behave itself.

And watch it putting forth each time to heaven,
Each time straight to heaven,
With marvelous naked assurance each single twig,
Each one setting off straight to the sky
As if it were the leader, the main-stem, the forerunner,
Intent to hold the candle of the sun upon its socket-tip,
It alone.

Every young twig
No sooner issued sideways from the thigh of his predecessor
Than off he starts without a qualm
To hold the one and only lighted candle of the sun in his socket-tip.
He casually gives birth to another young bud from his thigh,
Which at once sets off to be the one and only
And hold the lighted candle of the sun.

Oh many-branching candelabrum, oh strange up-starting fig-tree,
Oh weird Demos, where every twig is the arch twig!
Each imperiously over-equal to each, equality over-reaching itself
Like the snakes on Medusa's head
Oh naked fig-tree!

Still, no doubt every one of you can be the sun-socket as well as
        every other of you.
Demos, Demos, Demos!
Demon, too;
Wicked fig-tree, equality puzzle, with your self-conscious secret fruits.

Taormina

Bare Almond Trees

Wet almond trees, in the rain,
Like iron sticking grimly out of earth;
Black almond trunks, in the rain,
Like iron implements twisted, hideous, out of the earth,
Out of the deep, soft fledge of Sicilian winter-green,
Earth-grass uneatable,
Almond trunks curving blackly, iron-dark, climbing the slopes.

Almond tree, beneath the terrace rail,
Black, rusted, iron trunk,
You have welded your thin stems finer,
Like steel, like sensitive steel in the air,
Grey, lavender, sensitive steel, curving thinly and brittly up
        in a parabola.

What are you doing in the December rain?
Have you a strange electric sensitiveness in your steel tips?
Do you feel the air for electric influences
Like some strange magnetic apparatus?
Do you take in messages, in some strange code,
From heaven's wolfish, wandering electricity, that prowls so
        constantly round Etna?
Do you take the whisper of sulphur from the air?
Do you hear the chemical accents of the Sun?
Do you telephone the roar of the waters-over-the-earth?
And from all this, do you make calculations?

Sicily, December's Sicily in a mass of rain
With iron branching blackly, rusted like old, twisted implements
And brandishing and stooping over earth's wintry fledge, climbing
        the slopes
Of uneatable soft green!

Taormina

TROPIC

Sun, dark sun
Sun of black void heat
Sun of the torrid mid-day's horrific darkness

Behold my hair twisting and going black.
Behold my eyes turn tawny yellow
Negroid;
See the milk of northern spume
Coagulating and going black in my veins
Aromatic as frankincense.

Columns dark and soft
Sunblack men
Soft shafts, sunbreathing mouths
Eyes of yellow, golden sand
As frictional as perilous, explosive brimstone.

Rock, waves of dark heat;
Waves of dark heat, rock, sway upwards
Waver perpendicular.
What is the horizontal rolling of water
Compared to the flood of black heat that rolls upward past my eyes?

Taormina

SOUTHERN NIGHT

Come up, thou red thing.
Come up, and be called a moon.

The mosquitoes are biting tonight
Like memories.

Memories, northern memories,
Bitter-stinging white world that bore us
Subsiding into this night.

Call it moonrise
This red anathema?

Rise, thou red thing!
Unfold slowly upwards, blood-dark;
Burst the night's membrane of tranquil stars
Finally.

Maculate
The red Macula.

Taormina

FLOWERS

*"And long ago, the almond was the symbol of resurrection. But tell me,
tell me, why should the almond be the symbol of resurrection?
Have you not seen, in the wild winter sun of the southern Mediter-
ranean, in January and in February, the re-birth of the almond tree, all
standing in clouds of glory?
Ah yes! ah yes! would I might see it again!
Yet even this is not the secret of the secret. Do you know what was
called the almond bone, in the body, the last bone of the spine? This was
the seed of the body, and from the grave it could grow into a new body
again, like almond blossom in January.
No, no, I know nothing of that."*

*"Oh Persephone, Persephone, bring back to me from Hades the life
of a dead man."*

*"Wretches, utter wretches, keep your hands from beans!" saith Empedokles.
For according to some, the beans were the beans of votes, and votes
were politics. But others say it was a food-taboo. Others also say the
bean was one of the oldest symbols of the male organ, for the peas-cod
is later than the beans-cod."*

*"But blood is red, and blood is life. Red was the colour of kings. Kings, far-
off kings, painted their faces vermilion, and were almost gods."*

Almond Blossom

Even iron can put forth,
Even iron.

This is the iron age,
But let us take heart
Seeing iron break and bud,
Seeing rusty iron puff with clouds of blossom.

The almond tree,
December's bare iron hooks sticking out of earth.

The almond tree
That knows the deadliest poison, like a snake
In supreme bitterness.

Upon the iron, and upon the steel,
Odd flakes as if of snow, odd bits of snow,
Odd crumbs of melting snow.

But you mistake, it is not from the sky;
From out the iron, and from out the steel
Flying not down from heaven, but storming up,
Strange storming up from the dense under-earth
Along the iron, to the living steel
In rose-hot tips, and flakes of rose-pale snow
Setting supreme annunciation to the world.

Nay, what a heart of delicate super-faith,
Iron-breaking,
The rusty swords of almond trees.

FLOWERS

Trees suffer, like races, down the long ages.
They wander and are exiled, they live in exile through long ages
Like drawn blades never sheathed, hacked and gone black,
The alien trees in alien lands: and yet
The heart of blossom
The unquenchable heart of blossom!

Look at the many-cicatrised frail vine, none more scarred and frail;
Yet see him fling himself abroad in fresh abandon
From the small wound-stump.

Even the wilful, obstinate, gummy fig-tree
Can't be kept down, but he'll burst like a polyp into prolixity.

And the almond tree, in exile, in the iron age!

This is the ancient southern earth whence the vases were baked,
         amphoras, craters, cantharus, oenochoe and open-hearted cylix,
Bristling now with the iron of almond-trees.

Iron, but unforgetting
Iron, dawn-hearted
Ever-beating dawn-heart, enveloped in iron against the exile,
         against the ages.

See it come forth in blossom
From the snow-remembering heart
In long-nighted January,
In the long dark nights of the evenstar, and Sirius,
         and the Etna snow-wind through the long night.

Sweating his drops of blood through the long-nighted Gethsemane
Into blossom, into pride, into honey-triumph, into most
         exquisite splendour.

Oh, give me the tree of life in blossom
And the Cross sprouting its superb and fearless flowers!

Something must be reassuring to the almond, in the evening star,
    and the snow-wind, and the long, long nights,
Some memory of far, sun-gentler lands,
So that the faith in his heart smiles again
And his blood ripples with that untellable delight of once-more-
    vindicated faith,
And the Gethsemane blood at the iron pores unfolds, unfolds,
Pearls itself into tenderness of bud
And in a great and sacred forthcoming steps forth, steps out
    in one stride
A naked tree of blossom, like a bridegroom bathing in dew,
    divested of cover,
Frail-naked, utterly uncovered
To the green night-baying of the dog-star, Etna's snow-edged wind
And January's loud-seeming sun.

Think of it, from the iron fastness
Suddenly to dare to come out naked, in perfection of blossom,
    beyond the sword-rust.
Think, to stand there in full-unfolded nudity, smiling,
With all the snow-wind, and the sun-glare, and the dog-star
    baying epithalamion.

Oh, honey-bodied beautiful one
Come forth from iron
Red your heart is.
Fragile-tender, fragile-tender life-body
More fearless than iron all the time
And so much prouder, so disdainful of reluctances.

FLOWERS

In the distance like hoar-frost, like silvery ghosts communing
      on a green hill,
Hoar-frost-like and mysterious.

In the garden raying out
With a body like spray, dawn-tender, and looking about
With such insuperable, subtly-smiling assurance,
Sword-blade-born.

Unpromised,
No bounds being set.
Flaked out and come unpromised,
The tree being life-divine,
Fearing nothing, life-blissful at the core
Within iron and earth.

Knots of pink, fish-silvery
In heaven, in blue, blue heaven,
Soundless, blissful, wide-rayed, honey-bodied,
Red at the core
Red at the core
Knotted in heaven upon the fine light.

Open
Open
Five times wide open
Six times wide open
And given, and perfect;
And red at the core with the last sore-heartedness,
Sore-hearted-looking.

Fontana Vecchia

Purple Anemones

Who gave us flowers?
Heaven? The white God?

Nonsense!
Up out of hell
From Hades;
Infernal Dis!

Jesus the god of flowers—?
Not he.
Or sun-bright Apollo, him so musical?
Him neither.

Who then?
Say who.
Say it—and it is Pluto,
Dis
The dark one
Proserpine's master.

Who contradicts—?

When she broke forth from below,
Flowers came, hell-hounds on her heels.
Dis, the dark, the jealous god, the husband,
Flower-sumptuous-blooded.

Go then, he said.
And in Sicily, on the meadows of Enna,
She thought she had left him;
But opened around her purple anemones,

FLOWERS

Caverns,
Little hells of color, caves of darkness,
Hell, risen in pursuit of her; royal, sumptuous
Pit-falls.

All at her feet
Hell opening;
At her white ankles
Hell rearing its husband-splendid, serpent heads,
Hell-purple, to get at her—
Why did he let her go?
So he could track her down again, white victim.

Ah mastery!
Hell's husband-blossoms
Out on earth again.

Look out, Persephone!
You, Madame Ceres, mind yourself, the enemy is upon you.
About your feet spontaneous aconite,
Hell-glamorous, and purple husband-tyranny
Enveloping your late-enfranchised plains.

You thought your daughter had escaped?
No longer husband-hampered by the hell-lord, down in hell?
But ah my dear!

Aha, the stripe-checked whelps, whippet-slim crocuses!
At 'em, boys, at 'em!
Ho golden-spaniel, sweet alert narcissus,
Smell 'em, smell 'em out!
Those two enfranchised women.

FLOWERS

Somebody is coming!
Oho there!

Dark blue anemones!
Hell is up!
Hell on earth, and Dis within the depths!

Run, Persephone, he is after you already.

Why did he let her go?
To track her down;
All the sport of summer and spring, and flowers snapping
        at her ankles and catching her by the hair;
Poor Persephone and her rights for women.

Husband-snared hell-queen,
It is spring.

It is spring,
And pomp of husband-strategy on earth.

Ceres, kiss your girl, you think you've got her back.
The bit of husband-tilth she is,
Persephone!

Poor mothers-in-law!
They are always sold.

It is spring.

Taormina

Sicilian Cyclamens

When he pushed his bush of black hair off his brow:
When she lifted her mop from her eyes, and screwed it
    in a knob behind
    —O act of fearful temerity!
When they felt their foreheads bare, naked to heaven,
    their eyes revealed:
When they left the light of heaven brandished like a knife at
    their defenceless eyes
And the sea like a blade at their face,
Mediterranean savages:
When they came out, face-revealed, under heaven, from
    the shaggy undergrowth of their own hair
For the first time,
They saw tiny rose cyclamens between their toes, growing
Where the slow toads sat brooding on the past.

Slow toads, and cyclamen leaves
Stickily glistening with eternal shadow
Keeping to earth.
Cyclamen leaves
Toad-filmy, earth-iridescent
Beautiful
Frost-filigreed
Spumed with mud
Snail-nacreous
Low down.

The shaking aspect of the sea
And man's defenceless bare face
And cyclamens putting their ears back.

Long, pensive, slim-muzzled greyhound buds
Dreamy, not yet present,
Drawn out of earth
At his toes.

Dawn-rose
Sub-delighted, stone engendered
Cyclamens, young cyclamens
Arching
Waking, pricking their ears
Like delicate very-young greyhound bitches
Half-yawning at the open, inexperienced
Vistas of day,
Folding back their soundless petalled ears.

Greyhound bitches
Bending their rosy muzzles pensive down,
And breathing soft, unwilling to wake to the new day
Yet sub-delighted.

Ah Mediterranean morning, when our world began!
Far-off Mediterranean mornings,
Pelasgic faces uncovered
And unbudding cyclamens.

The hare suddenly goes uphill
Laying back her long ears with unwinking bliss.

And up the pallid, sea-blenched Mediterranean stone-slopes
Rose cyclamen, ecstatic fore-runner!
Cyclamens, ruddy-muzzled cyclamens
In little bunches like bunches of wild hares
Muzzles together, ears-aprick

FLOWERS

Whispering witchcraft
Like women at a well, the dawn-fountain.

Greece, and the world's morning
While all the Parthenon marbles still fostered the roots of the cyclamen.
Violets
Pagan, rosy-muzzled violets
Autumnal
Dawn-pink,
Dawn-pale
Among squat toad-leaves sprinkling the unborn
Erechtheion marbles.

Taormina

Hibiscus and Salvia Flowers

Hark! Hark!
The dogs do bark!
It's the socialists come to town,
None in rags and none in tags,
Swaggering up and down.

Sunday morning,
And from the Sicilian townlets skirting Etna
The Socialists have gathered upon us, to look at us.

How shall we know them when we see them?
How shall we know them now they've come?

Not by their rags and not by their tags
Nor by any reproachful gown;
The same unremarkable Sunday suit
And hats cocked up and down.

Yet there they are, youths, loutishly
Strolling in gangs and staring along the Corso
With the gang-stare
And a half-threatening envy
At every *forestiere*,
Every lordly tuppenny foreigner from the hotels, fattening
      on the exchange.

Hark! Hark!
The dogs do bark!
It's the socialists in the town.

FLOWERS

Sans rags, sans tags,
Sans beards, sans bags,
Sans any distinction at all except loutish commonness.

How do we know then, that they are they?
Bolshevists.
Leninists.
Communists.
Socialists.
-Ists! -Ists!

Alas, salvia and hibiscus flowers.
Salvia and hibiscus flowers.

Listen again.
Salvia and hibiscus flowers.
Is it not so?
Salvia and hibiscus flowers.

Hark! Hark!
The dogs do bark!
Salvia and hibiscus flowers.

Who smeared their doors with blood?
Who on their breasts
Put salvias and hibiscus?

Rosy, rosy scarlet,
And flame-rage, golden throated
Bloom along the Corso on the living, perambulating bush.

Who said they might assume these blossoms?
What god did they consult?

48

Rose-red, princess hibiscus, rolling her pointed Chinese petals!
Azalea and camellia, single peony
And pomegranate bloom and scarlet mallow-flower
And all the eastern, exquisite royal plants
That noble blood has brought us down the ages!
Gently-nurtured, frail and splendid
Hibiscus flower—
Alas, the Sunday coats of Sicilian bolshevists!

Pure blood, and noble blood, in the fine and rose-red veins;
Small, interspersed with jewels of white gold
Frail-filigreed among the rest;
Rose of the oldest races of princesses, Polynesian hibiscus.

Eve, in her happy moments,
Put hibiscus in her hair,
Before she took to knowledge, before she spoilt it all by knowing better.

Sicilian bolshevists
With hibiscus flowers in the buttonholes of your Sunday suits,
Come now, speaking of rights, what right have you to this flower?

The exquisite and ageless aristocracy
Of a peerless soul!
Blessed are the pure in heart and the fathomless in bright pride!
The loveliness that knows *noblesse oblige*;
The natural royalty of red hibiscus flowers;
The exquisite assertions of pure life
Risen from the roots:
Have it this way, will you, red-decked socialists,
Hibiscus-breasted?

FLOWERS

If it be so, I fly to join you,
And if it be not so, who are you, to pull down hibiscus flowers!

Or salvia!
Or dragon-mouthed salvia with gold throat of wrath!
Flame-flushed, enraged, splendid salvia,
Cock-crested, crowing your orange scarlet like a tocsin
Along the Corso all this Sunday morning.

Is your wrath red as salvias',
You socialists?
You with your grudging, envious, furtive rage,
In Sunday suits and yellow boots along the Corso,
Salvia flowers become you, I must say.

Warrior-like, dawn-cock's-comb flaring flower
Shouting forth flame to set the world on fire,
The dust-heap of man's filthy world on fire,
And burn it down, the glutted, stuffy world,
And feed the young new fields of life with ash
With ash I say,
Bolshevists,
Your ashes even, my friends,
Among much other ash.

If there were salvia-savage bolshevists
To burn the world back to manure-good ash,
Wouldn't I stick the salvia in my coat!
But these themselves must burn, these louts!

The dragon-faced,
The anger-reddened, furious-throated salvia
With its long antennae of rage put out

Upon the frightened air.
Ugh, how I love its fangs of perfect rage
That gnash the air;
The molten gold of its intolerable rage
Hot in the throat.

I long to be a bolshevist
And set the stinking rubbish-heap of this foul world
Afire at a myriad scarlet points,
A bolshevist, a salvia-face
To lick the world with flame that licks it clean.

I long to see its chock-full crowdedness
And glutted squirming populousness on fire
Like a field of filthy weeds
Burnt back to ash,
And then to see the new, real souls sprout up.
Not this vast rotting cabbage-patch we call the world;
But from the ash-scarred fallow
New wild souls.

Nettles, and a rose sprout,
Hibiscus, and mere grass,
Salvia still in a rage
And almond honey-still,
And fig-wort stinking for the carrion wasp;
All the lot of them, and let each hold his own.

Without a trace of foul equality,
None of them holding more than is his own.
You need not clear the world like a cabbage-patch for me;
Leave me my nettles,

FLOWERS

Let me fight the wicked, obstreperous weeds myself, and put them
     in their place, and keep them there;
I don't at all want to annihilate them,
I like the fight with them,
But I won't be put on a cabbage-idealistic level of equality with them.

What rot, to see the cabbage and hibiscus tree
As equals!
What rot, to say the louts along the Corso
In Sunday suits and yellow shoes
Are my equals!
I am their superior, saluting the hibiscus flower, not them.
The same I say to the profiteers from the hotels, the money-fat-ones,
Profiteers here being called dog-fish, stinking dog-fish, sharks.
The same I say to the pale and elegant persons,
Pale-face authorities loitering tepidly:
That I salute the red hibiscus flowers
And send mankind to its inferior blazes,
Mankind's inferior blazes,
And these along with it, all the inferior lot—
These bolshevists,
These dog-fish,
These precious and ideal ones,
All rubbish ready for fire.

And I salute hibiscus and the salvia flower
Upon the breasts of loutish bolshevists,
Damned loutish bolshevists,
Who perhaps will do the business after all,
In the long run, in spite of themselves.

Meanwhile, alas
For me no fellow-men,

No salvia-frenzied comrades, antennae
Of yellow-red, outreaching, living wrath
Upon the smouldering air,
And throat of brimstone-molten angry gold.
Red, angry men are a race extinct, alas!

Never
To be a bolshevist
With a hibiscus flower behind my ear
In sign of life, of lovely, dangerous life
And passionate disquality of men;
In sign of dauntless, silent violets,
And impudent nettles grabbing the under-earth,
And cabbages born to be cut and eat,
And salvia fierce to crow and shout for fight,
And rosy red hibiscus wincingly
Unfolding all her coiled and lovely self
In a doubtful world.

Never, bolshevistically
To be able to stand for all these!
Alas, alas, I have got to leave it all
To the youths in Sunday suits and yellow shoes
Who have pulled down the salvia flowers
And rosy delicate hibiscus flowers
And everything else to their disgusting level,
Never, of course, to put anything up again.

But yet
If they pull all the world down,
The process will amount to the same in the end.
Instead of flame and flame-clean ash
Slow watery rotting back to level muck

FLOWERS

And final humus,
Whence the re-start.

And still I cannot bear it
That they take hibiscus and the salvia flower.

Taormina

THE EVANGELISTIC BEASTS

"Oh put them back, put them back in the four corners of the heavens,
where they belong, the Apocalyptic beasts. For with their wings full of
stars they rule the night, and man that watches through the night lives
four lives, and man that sleeps through the night sleeps four sleeps,
the sleep of the lion, the sleep of the bull, the sleep of the man, and the
eagle's sleep. After which the lion wakes, and it is day. Then from the
four quarters the four winds blow, and life has its changes. But when
the heavens are empty, empty of the four great Beasts, the four Natures,
the four Winds, the four Quarters, then sleep is empty too, man sleeps no
more like the lion and the bull, nor wakes from the light-eyed eagle sleep."

St. Matthew

They are not all beasts.
One is a man, for example, and one is a bird.

I, Matthew, am a man.

"And I, if I be lifted up, will draw all men unto me—"

This Jesus.
But then Jesus was not quite a man.
He was the Son of Man
Filius Meus, O remorseless logic
Out of His own mouth.

I, Matthew, being a man
Cannot be lifted up, the Paraclete,
To draw all men unto me,
Seeing I am on a par with all men.

I, on the other hand,
Am drawn to the Uplifted, as all men are drawn,
To the Son of Man
Filius Meus.

Wilt thou lift me up, Son of Man?
How my heart beats!
I am man.

I am man, and therefore my heart beats, and throws the dark blood
        from side to side
All the time I am lifted up.

Yes, even during my uplifting.

THE EVANGELISTIC BEASTS

And if it ceased?

If it ceased, I should be no longer man

As I am, if my heart in uplifting ceased to beat, to toss the dark blood
from side to side, causing my myriad secret streams.

After the cessation

I might be a soul in bliss, an angel, approximating to the Uplifted;

But that is another matter;

I am Matthew, the man,

And I am not that other angelic matter.

So I will be lifted up, Saviour,

But put me down again in time, Master,

Before my heart stops beating, and I become what I am not.

Put me down again on the earth, Jesus, on the brown soil

Where flowers sprout in the acrid humus, and fade into humus again.

Where beasts drop their unlicked young, and pasture, and drop their
droppings among the turf.

Where the adder darts horizontal.

Down on the damp, unceasing ground, where my feet belong

And even my heart, Lord, forever, after all uplifting:

The crumbling, damp, fresh land, life horizontal and ceaseless.

Matthew I am, the man.

And I take the wings of the morning, to Thee, Crucified, Glorified.

But while flowers club their petals at evening

And rabbits make pills among the short grass

And long snakes quickly glide into the dark hole in the wall,
hearing man approach,

I must be put down, Lord, in the afternoon,

And at evening I must leave off my wings of the spirit

As I leave off my braces

And I must resume my nakedness like a fish, sinking down
the dark reversion of night

THE EVANGELISTIC BEASTS

Like a fish seeking the bottom, Jesus,
ΙΧΘΥΣ
Face downwards
Veering slowly
Down between the steep slopes of darkness, fucus-dark,
        seaweed-fringed valleys of the waters under the sea
Over the edge of the soundless cataract
Into the fathomless, bottomless pit
Where my soul falls in the last throes of bottomless convulsion,
        and is fallen
Utterly beyond Thee, Dove of the Spirit;
Beyond everything, except itself.

Nay, Son of Man, I have been lifted up.
To Thee I rose like a rocket ending in mid-heaven.
But even Thou, Son of Man, canst not quaff out the dregs of
        terrestrial manhood!
They fall back from Thee.

They fall back, and like a dripping of quicksilver taking
        the downward track,
Break into drops, burn into drops of blood, and dropping, dropping
        take wing
Membraned, blood-veined wings.
On fans of unsuspected tissue, like bats
They thread and thrill and flicker ever downward
To the dark zenith of Thine antipodes
Jesus Uplifted.

Bat-winged heart of man
Reversed flame
Shuddering a strange way down the bottomless pit
To the great depths of its reversèd zenith.

THE EVANGELISTIC BEASTS

Afterwards, afterwards
Morning comes, and I shake the dews of night from the wings
    of my spirit
And mount like a lark, Beloved.

But remember, Saviour,
That my heart which like a lark at heaven's gate singing, hovers
    morning-bright to Thee,
Throws still the dark blood back and forth
In the avenues where the bat hangs sleeping, upside-down
And to me undeniable, Jesus.

Listen, Paraclete.
I can no more deny the bat-wings of my fathom-flickering spirit
    of darkness
Than the wings of the Morning and Thee, Thou Glorified.

I am Matthew, the Man:
It is understood.
And Thou art Jesus, Son of Man
Drawing all men unto Thee, but bound to release them when
    the hour strikes.

I have been, and I have returned.
I have mounted up on the wings of the morning, and I have
    dredged down to the zenith's reversal.
Which is my way, being man.
Gods may stay in mid-heaven, the Son of Man has climbed
    to the Whitsun zenith,
But I, Matthew, being a man
Am a traveller back and forth.
So be it.

St. Mark

There was a lion in Judah
Which whelped, and was Mark.

But winged.
A lion with wings.
At least in Venice.
Even as late as Daniele Manin.

Why should he have wings?
Is he to be a bird also?
Or a spirit?
Or a winged thought?
Or a soaring consciousness?

Evidently he is all that
The lion of the spirit.

Ah, Lamb of God
Would a wingless lion lie down before Thee, as this winged lion lies?

The lion of the spirit.

Once he lay in the mouth of a cave
And sunned his whiskers,
And lashed his tail slowly, slowly
Thinking of voluptuousness
Even of blood.

But later, in the sun of the afternoon
Having tasted all there was to taste, and having slept his fill

THE EVANGELISTIC BEASTS

He fell to frowning, as he lay with his head on his paws
And the sun coming in through the narrowest fibril of a slit
    in his eyes.

So nine-tenths asleep, motionless, bored, and statically angry,
He saw in a shaft of light a lamb on a pinnacle, balancing a flag
    on its paw,
And he was thoroughly startled.

Going out to investigate
He found the lamb beyond him, on the inaccessible pinnacle of light.
So he put his paw to his nose, and pondered.

"Guard my sheep," came the silvery voice from the pinnacle,
"And I will give thee the wings of the morning."
So the lion of blood thought it was worth it.

Hence he became a curly sheep-dog with dangerous propensities
As Carpaccio will tell you:
Ramping round, guarding the flock of mankind,
Sharpening his teeth on the wolves,
Ramping up through the air like a kestrel
And lashing his tail above the world
And enjoying the sensation of heaven and righteousness
    and voluptuous wrath.

There is a new sweetness in his voluptuously licking his paw
Now that it is a weapon of heaven.
There is a new ecstasy in his roar of desirous love
Now that it sounds self-conscious through the unlimited sky.
He is well aware of himself
And he cherishes voluptuous delights, and thinks about them
And ceases to be a blood-thirsty king of beasts

And becomes the faithful sheep-dog of the Shepherd, thinking
    of his voluptuous pleasures of chasing the sheep to the fold
And increasing the flock, and perhaps giving a real nip here and there,
    a real pinch, but always well meant.

And somewhere there is a lioness
The she-mate.
Whelps play between the paws of the lion,
The she-mate purrs
Their castle is impregnable, their cave,
The sun comes in their lair, they are well-off,
A well-to-do family.

Then the proud lion stalks abroad, alone
And roars to announce himself to the wolves
And also to encourage the red-cross Lamb
And chiefly to ensure a goodly increase in the world.

Look at him, with his paw on the world
At Venice and elsewhere.
Going blind at last.

St. Luke

A wall, a bastion,
A living forehead with its slow whorl of hair
And a bull's large, sombre, glancing eye
And glistening, adhesive muzzle
With cavernous nostrils where the winds run hot
Snorting defiance,
Or greedily snuffing behind the cows.

Horns
The golden horns of power,
Power to kill, power to create
Such as Moses had, and God,
Head-power.

Shall great wings flame from his shoulder sockets
Assyrian-wise?
It would be no wonder.

Knowing the thunder of his heart
The massive thunder of his dew-lapped chest
Deep and reverberating,
It would be no wonder if great wings, like flame, fanned out
        from the furnace-cracks of his shoulder-sockets.

Thud! Thud! Thud!
And the roar of black bull's blood in the mighty passages of his chest.

Ah, the dewlap swings pendulous with excess.
The great, roaring weight above
Like a furnace dripping a molten drip.

The urge, the massive, burning ache
Of the bull's breast.
The open furnace-doors of his nostrils.

For what does he ache, and groan?

Is his breast a wall?

Nay, once it was also a fortress wall, and the weight of a vast battery.
But now it is a burning hearthstone only,
Massive old altar of his own burnt offering.

It was always an altar of burnt offering
His own black blood poured out like a sheet of flame over
      his fecundating herd
As he gave himself forth.

But also it was a fiery fortress frowning shaggily on the world
And announcing battle ready.

Since the Lamb bewitched him with that red-struck flag
His fortress is dismantled
His fires of wrath are banked down
His horns turn away from the enemy.

He serves the Son of Man.

And hear him bellow, after many years, the bull that serves
      the Son of Man.
Moaning, booing, roaring hollow
Constrained to pour forth all his fire down the narrow sluice
      of procreation
Through such narrow loins, too narrow.

THE EVANGELISTIC BEASTS

Is he not over-charged by the dammed-up pressure of his own
    massive black blood
Luke, the Bull, the father of substance, the Providence Bull,
    after two thousand years?
Is he not over-full of offering, a vast, a vast offer of himself
Which must be poured through so small a vent?

Too small a vent.

Let him remember his horns, then.
Seal up his forehead once more to a bastion,
Let it know nothing.
Let him charge like a mighty catapult on the red-cross flag,
    let him roar out challenge on the world.
And throwing himself upon it, throw off the madness of his blood.
Let it be war.

And so it is war.
The bull of the proletariat has got his head down.

St. John

John, Oh John,
Thou honourable bird
Sun-peering eagle.

Taking a bird's-eye view
Even of Calvary and Resurrection
Not to speak of Babylon's whoredom.

High over the mild effulgence of the dove
Hung all the time, did we but know it, the all-knowing shadow
Of John's great gold-barred eagle.

John knew all about it
Even the very beginning.

"In the beginning was the Word
And the word was God
And the Word was with God."

Having been to school
John knew the whole proposition.
As for innocent Jesus
He was one of Nature's phenomena, no doubt.

Oh that mind-soaring eagle of an Evangelist
Staring creation out of countenance
And telling it off
As an eagle staring down on the Sun!

The Logos, the Logos!
"In the beginning was the Word."

THE EVANGELISTIC BEASTS

Is there not a great Mind pre-ordaining?
Does not a supreme Intellect ideally procreate the Universe?
Is not each soul a vivid thought in the great consciousness-stream
    of God?

Put salt on his tail
The sly bird of John.

Proud intellect, high-soaring Mind
Like a king eagle, bird of the most High, sweeping the round of heaven
And casting the cycles of creation
On two wings, like a pair of compasses;
Jesus' pale and lambent dove, cooing in the lower boughs
On sufferance.

In the beginning was the Word, of course.
And the word was the first offspring of the almighty Johannine mind,
Chick of the intellectual eagle.

Yet put salt on the tail of the Johannine bird
Put salt on its tail
John's eagle.

Shoo it down out of the empyrean
Of the all-seeing, all-fore-ordaining ideal.
Make it roost on bird-spattered, rocky Patmos
And let it moult there, among the stones of the bitter sea.

For the almighty eagle of the fore-ordaining Mind
Is looking rather shabby and island-bound these days;
Moulting, and rather naked about the rump, and down in the beak,
Rather dirty, on dung-whitened Patmos.

From which we are led to assume
That the old bird is weary, and almost willing
That a new chick should chip the extensive shell
Of the mundane egg.

The poor old golden eagle of the creative spirit
Moulting and moping and waiting, willing at last
For the fire to burn it up, feathers and all
So that a new conception of the beginning and end
Can rise from the ashes.

Ah Phoenix, Phoenix
John's Eagle!
You are only known to us now as the badge of an insurance Company.

Phoenix, Phoenix
The nest is in flames
Feathers are singeing,
Ash flutters flocculent, like down on a blue, wan fledgeling.

San Gervasio

CREATURES

"But fishes are very fiery and take to the water to cool themselves."
"To those things that love darkness, the light of day is cruel and a pain.
Yet the light of lamps and candles has no fears for them; rather they
draw near to taste it, as if saying: Now what is this? So we see that the
sun is more than burning, more than the burning of fires or the shining
of lamps. Because with his rays he hurts the creatures that live by night,
and lamplight and firelight do them no hurt. Therefore the sun lives in
his shining, and is not like fires, that die."

Mosquito

When did you start your tricks
Monsieur?

What do you stand on such high legs for?
Why this length of shredded shank
You exaltation?

Is it so that you shall lift your centre of gravity upwards
And weigh no more than air as you alight upon me,
Stand upon me weightless, you phantom?

I heard a woman call you the Winged Victory
In sluggish Venice.
You turn your head towards your tail, and smile.

How can you put so much devilry
Into that translucent phantom shred
Of a frail corpus?

Queer, with your thin wings and your streaming legs
How you sail like a heron, or a dull clot of air,
A nothingness.

Yet what an aura surrounds you;
Your evil little aura, prowling, and casting a numbness on my mind.

That is your trick, your bit of filthy magic:
Invisibility, and the anaesthetic power
To deaden my attention in your direction.

But I know your game now, streaky sorcerer.

CREATURES

Queer, how you stalk and prowl the air
In circles and evasions, enveloping me,
Ghoul on wings
Winged Victory.

Settle, and stand on long thin shanks
Eyeing me sideways, and cunningly conscious that I am aware,
You speck.
I hate the way you lurch off sideways into air
Having read my thoughts against you.

Come then, let us play at unawares
And see who wins in this sly game of bluff,
Man or mosquito.
You don't know that I exist, and I don't know that you exist.
Now then!

It is your trump.
It is your hateful little trump,
You pointed fiend,
Which shakes my sudden blood to hatred of you:
It is your small, high, hateful bugle in my ear.

Why do you do it?
Surely it is bad policy.

They say you can't help it.

If that is so, then I believe a little in Providence protecting the innocent.
But it sounds so amazingly like a slogan,
A yell of triumph as you snatch my scalp.

Blood, red blood
Super-magical
Forbidden liquor.

CREATURES

I behold you stand
For a second enspasmed in oblivion,
Obscenely ecstasied
Sucking live blood,
My blood.

Such silence, such suspended transport,
Such gorging,
Such obscenity of trespass.

You stagger
As well you may.
Only your accursed hairy frailty
Your own imponderable weightlessness
Saves you, wafts you away on the very draught my anger makes
       in its snatching.

Away with a paean of derision
You winged blood-drop.

Can I not overtake you?
Are you one too many for me
Winged Victory?
Am I not mosquito enough to out-mosquito you?

Queer, what a big stain my sucked blood makes
Beside the infinitesimal faint smear of you!
Queer, what a dim dark smudge you have disappeared into!

Siracusa

Fish

Fish, oh Fish,
So little matters!

Whether the waters rise and cover the earth
Or whether the waters wilt in the hollow places,
All one to you.

Aqueous, subaqueous,
Submerged
And wave-thrilled.

As the waters roll
Roll you.
The waters wash,
You wash in oneness
And never emerge.

Never know,
Never grasp.

Your life a sluice of sensation along your sides,
A flush at the flails of your fins, down the whorl of your tail,
And water wetly on fire in the grates of your gills;
Fixed water-eyes.

Even snakes lie together.

But oh, fish, that rock in water,
You lie only with the waters;
One touch.

CREATURES

No fingers, no hands and feet, no lips;
No tender muzzles,
No wistful bellies,
No loins of desire,
None.

You and the naked element,
Sway-wave.
Curvetting bits of tin in the evening light.

Who is it ejects his sperm to the naked flood?
In the wave-mother?
Who swims enwombed?
Who lies with the waters of his silent passion, womb-element?
—Fish in the waters under the earth.

What price *his* bread upon the waters?

Himself all silvery himself
In the element
No more.

Nothing more.

Himself,
And the element.
Food, of course!
Water-eager eyes,
Mouth-gate open
And strong spine urging, driving;
And desirous belly gulping.

Fear also!
He knows fear!

CREATURES

Water-eyes craning,
A rush that almost screams,
Almost fish-voice
As the pike comes. . . .
Then gay fear, that turns the tail sprightly, from a shadow.

Food, and fear, and joie de vivre,
Without love.

The other way about:
Joie de vivre, and fear, and food,
All without love.

Quelle joie de vivre
Dans l'eau!
Slowly to gape through the waters,
Alone with the element;
To sink, and rise, and go to sleep with the waters;
To speak endless inaudible wavelets into the wave;
To breathe from the flood at the gills,
Fish-blood slowly running next to the flood, extracting fish-fire;
To have the element under one, like a lover;
And to spring away with a curvetting click in the air,
Provocative.
Dropping back with a slap on the face of the flood.
And merging oneself!

To be a fish!

So utterly without misgiving
To be a fish
In the waters.

Loveless, and so lively!
Born before God was love,

Or life knew loving.
Beautifully beforehand with it all.

Admitted, they swarm in companies,
Fishes.
They drive in shoals.
But soundless, and out of contact.
They exchange no word, no spasm, not even anger.
Not one touch.
Many suspended together, forever apart,
Each one alone with the waters, upon one wave with the rest.

A magnetism in the water between them only.

I saw a water-serpent swim across the Anapo,
And I said to my heart, *look, look at him!*
With his head up, steering like a bird!
He's a rare one, but he belongs. . . .

But sitting in a boat on the Zeller lake
And watching the fishes in the breathing waters
Lift and swim and go their way—

I said to my heart, *who are these?*
And my heart couldn't own them. . . .

A slim young pike, with smart fins
And grey-striped suit, a young cub of a pike
Slouching along away below, half out of sight,
Like a lout on an obscure pavement. . . .

Aha, there's somebody in the know!

But watching closer
That motionless deadly motion,

CREATURES

That unnatural barrel body, that long ghoul nose . . .
I left off hailing him.

I had made a mistake, I didn't know him,
This grey, monotonous soul in the water,
This intense individual in shadow,
Fish-alive.

I didn't know his God,
I didn't know his God.

Which is perhaps the last admission that life has to wring out of us.

I saw, dimly,
Once a big pike rush,
And small fish fly like splinters.
And I said to my heart, *there are limits*
To you, my heart;
And to the one God.
Fish are beyond me.

Other Gods
Beyond my range . . . gods beyond my God. . . .

They are beyond me, are fishes.
I stand at the pale of my being
And look beyond, and see
Fish, in the outerwards,
As one stands on a bank and looks in.

I have waited with a long rod
And suddenly pulled a gold-and-greenish, lucent fish from below,
And had him fly like a halo round my head,
Lunging in the air on the line.

Unhooked his gorping, water-horny mouth,
And seen his horror-tilted eye,
His red-gold, water-precious, mirror-flat bright eye;
And felt him beat in my hand, with his mucous, leaping lifethrob.

And my heart accused itself
Thinking: *I am not the measure of creation.*
This is beyond me, this fish.
His God stands outside my God.

And the gold-and-green pure lacquer-mucous comes off in my hand,
And the red-gold mirror-eye stares and dies,
And the water-suave contour dims.

But not before I have had to know
He was born in front of my sunrise,
Before my day.

He outstarts me.
And I, a many-fingered horror of daylight to him,
Have made him die.

Fishes,
With their gold, red eyes, and green-pure gleam, and under-gold,
And their pre-world loneliness,
And more than lovelessness,
And white meat;
They move in other circles.

Outsiders.
Water-wayfarers.
Things of one element.
Aqueous,
Each by itself.

CREATURES

Cats, and the Neapolitans,
Sulphur sun-beasts,
Thirst for fish as for more-than-water;
Water-alive
To quench their over-sulphureous lusts.

But I, I only wonder
And don't know.
I don't know fishes.

In the beginning
Jesus was called The Fish. . . .
And in the end.

Zell-am-See

Bat

At evening, sitting on this terrace,
When the sun from the west, beyond Pisa, beyond the mountains
    of Carrara
Departs, and the world is taken by surprise . . .

When the tired flower of Florence is in gloom beneath the glowing
Brown hills surrounding . . .

When under the arches of the Ponte Vecchio
A green light enters against-stream, flush from the west,
Against the current of obscure Arno . . .

Look up, and you see things flying
Between the day and the night;
Swallows with spools of dark thread sewing the shadows together.

A circle swoop, and a quick parabola under the bridge arches
Where light pushes through;
A sudden turning upon itself of a thing in the air.
A dip to the water.

And you think:
"The swallows are flying so late!"

Swallows?

Dark air-life looping
Yet missing the pure loop . . .
A twitch, a twitter, an elastic shudder in flight
And serrated wings against the sky,

CREATURES

Like a glove, a black glove thrown up at the light
And falling back.

Never swallows!
Bats!
The swallows are gone.

At a wavering instant the swallows gave way to bats
By the Ponte Vecchio...
Changing guard.

Bats, and an uneasy creeping in one's scalp
As the bats swoop overhead!
Flying madly.

Pipistrello!
Black piper on an infinitesimal pipe.
Little lumps that fly in air and have voices indefinite, wildly vindictive;
Wings like bits of umbrella.

Bats!

Creatures that hang themselves up like an old rag, to sleep;
And disgustingly upside down.

Hanging upside down like rows of disgusting old rags
And grinning in their sleep.
Bats!

In China the bat is symbol of happiness.

Not for me!

Florence

Man and Bat

When I went into my room, at midmorning,
Say ten o'clock . . .
My room, a crash-box over that great stone rattle
The Via de' Bardi . . .

When I went into my room at mid-morning
Why? . . . a bird!

A bird
Flying round the room in insane circles.

In insane circles!
. . . *A bat!*

A disgusting bat
At mid-morning! . . .

Out! Go out!

Round and round and round
With a twitchy, nervous, intolerable flight,
And a neurasthenic lunge,
And an impure frenzy;
A bat, big as a swallow!

Out, out of my room!

The Venetian shutters I push wide
To the free, calm upper air;
Loop back the curtains . . .

CREATURES

Now out, out from my room!

So to drive him out, flicking with my white handkerchief: *Go!*
But he will not.

Round and round and round
In an impure haste,
Fumbling, a beast in air,
And stumbling, lunging and touching the walls, the bell-wires
About my room!

Always refusing to go out into the air
Above that crash-gulf of the Via de' Bardi,
Yet blind with frenzy, with cluttered fear.
At last he swerved into the window bay,
But blew back, as if an incoming wind blew him in again.
A strong inrushing wind.

And round and round and round!
Blundering more insane, and leaping, in throbs, to clutch at a corner,
At a wire, at a bell-rope:
On and on, watched relentless by me, round and round in my room,
Round and round and dithering with tiredness and haste
        and increasing delirium
Flicker-splashing round my room.

I would not let him rest;
Not one instant cleave, cling like a blot with his breast to the wall
In an obscure corner.
Not an instant!

I flicked him on,
Trying to drive him through the window.

Again he swerved into the window bay
And I ran forward, to frighten him forth.
But he rose, and from a terror worse than me he flew past me
Back into my room, and round, round, round in my room
Clutch, cleave, stagger,
Dropping about the air
Getting tired.

Something seemed to blow him back from the window
Every time he swerved at it;
Back on a strange parabola, then round, round, dizzy in my room.

He *could* not go out;
I also realised. . . .

It was the light of day which he could not enter,
Any more than I could enter the white-hot door of a blast-furnace.
He could not plunge into the daylight that streamed at the window.
It was asking too much of his nature.

Worse even than the hideous terror of me with my handkerchief
Saying: *Out, go out!* . . .
Was the horror of white daylight in the window!

So I switched on the electric light, thinking: *Now*
The outside will seem brown. . . .

But no.
The outside did not seem brown.
And he did not mind the yellow electric light.

Silent!
He was having a silent rest.
But never!
Not in my room.

87

CREATURES

Round and round and round
Near the ceiling as if in a web,
Staggering;
Plunging, falling out of the web,
Broken in heaviness,
Lunging blindly,
Heavier;
And clutching, clutching for one second's pause,
Always, as if for one drop of rest,
One little drop.

And I!
Never, I say. . . .
Go out!

Flying slower,
Seeming to stumble, to fall in air.
Blind-weary.

Yet never able to pass the whiteness of light into freedom. . . .
A bird would have dashed through, come what might.

Fall, sink, lurch, and round and round
Flicker, flicker-heavy;
Even wings heavy:
And cleave in a high corner for a second, like a clot, also a prayer.

But no.
Out, you beast.

Till he fell in a corner, palpitating, spent.
And there, a clot, he squatted and looked at me.
With sticking-out, bead-berry eyes, black,

And improper derisive ears,
And shut wings,
And brown, furry body.

Brown, nut-brown, fine fur!
But it might as well have been hair on a spider; thing
With long, black-paper ears.

So, a dilemma!
He squatted there like something unclean.

No, he must not squat, nor hang, obscene, in my room!

Yet nothing on earth will give him courage to pass the sweet fire of
day.

What then?
Hit him and kill him and throw him away?

Nay,
I didn't create him.
Let the God that created him be responsible for his death. . . .
Only, in the bright day, I will not have this clot in my room.

Let the God who is maker of bats watch with them in their
        unclean corners. . . .
I admit a God in every crevice,
But not bats in my room;
Nor the God of bats, while the sun shines.

So out, out you brute! . . .
And he lunged, flight-heavy, away from me, sideways, *a sghembo!*
And round and round and round my room, a clot with wings,
Impure even in weariness.

CREATURES

Wings dark skinny and flapping the air,
Lost their flicker.
Spent.

He fell again with a little thud
Near the curtain on the floor.
And there lay.

Ah, death, death,
You are no solution!
Bats must be bats.

Only life has a way out.
And the human soul is fated to wide-eyed responsibility
In life.

So I picked him up in a flannel jacket,
Well covered, lest he should bite me.
For I would have had to kill him if he'd bitten me, the impure one. . . .
And he hardly stirred in my hand, muffled up.

Hastily, I shook him out of the window.

And away he went!
Fear craven in his tail.
Great haste, and straight, almost bird-straight above the Via de' Bardi.
Above that crash-gulf of exploding whips,
Towards the Borgo San Jacopo.

And now, at evening, as he flickers over the river
Dipping with petty triumphant flight, and tittering over
        the sun's departure,

CREATURES

I believe he chirps, pipistrello, seeing me here on this terrace writing:
There he sits, the long loud one!
But I am greater than he . . .
I escaped him. . . .

Florence

REPTILES

"Homer was wrong in saying 'would that strife might pass away from among gods and men!' He did not see that he was praying for the destruction of the universe; for, if his prayer were heard, all things would pass away—for in the tension of opposites all things have their being—."

"For when Fire in its downward path chanced to mingle with the dark breath of the earth, the serpent slid forth, lay revealed. But he was moist and cold, the sun in him darted uneasy, held down by moist earth, never could he rise on his feet. And this is what put poison in his mouth. For the sun in him would fain rise half-way, and move on feet. But moist earth weighs him down, though he dart and twist, still he must go with his belly on the ground.—The wise tortoise laid his earthy part around him, he cast it round him and found his feet. So he is the first of creatures to stand upon his toes, and the dome of his house is his heaven. Therefore it is charted out, and is the foundation of the world."

Snake

A snake came to my water-trough
On a hot, hot day, and I in pyjamas for the heat,
To drink there.

In the deep, strange-scented shade of the great dark carob tree
I came down the steps with my pitcher
And must wait, must stand and wait, for there he was at the trough
      before me.

He reached down from a fissure in the earth-wall in the gloom
And trailed his yellow-brown slackness soft-bellied down, over
      the edge of the stone trough
And rested his throat upon the stone bottom,
And where the water had dripped from the tap, in a small clearness,
He sipped with his straight mouth,
Softly drank through his straight gums, into his slack long body,
Silently.

Someone was before me at my water-trough,
And I, like a second-comer, waiting.

He lifted his head from his drinking, as cattle do,
And looked at me vaguely, as drinking cattle do,
And flickered his two-forked tongue from his lips, and mused
      a moment,
And stooped and drank a little more,
Being earth-brown, earth-golden from the burning bowels
      of the earth
On the day of Sicilian July, with Etna smoking.

REPTILES

The voice of my education said to me
He must be killed,
For in Sicily the black, black snakes are innocent, the gold
    are venomous.

And voices in me said, If you were a man
You would take a stick and break him now, and finish him off.

But must I confess how I liked him,
How glad I was he had come like a guest in quiet, to drink
    at my water-trough
And depart peaceful, pacified, and thankless,
Into the burning bowels of this earth?

Was it cowardice, that I dared not kill him?
Was it perversity, that I longed to talk to him?
Was it humility, to feel so honoured?
I felt so honoured.

And yet those voices:
If you were not afraid, you would kill him!

And truly I was afraid, I was most afraid,
But even so, honoured still more
That he should seek my hospitality
From out the dark door of the secret earth.

He drank enough
And lifted his head, dreamily, as one who has drunken,
And flickered his tongue like a forked night on the air, so black,
Seeming to lick his lips,
And looked around like a god, unseeing, into the air,
And slowly turned his head,
And slowly, very slowly, as if thrice adream

Proceeded to draw his slow length curving round
And climb again the broken bank of my wall-face.

And as he put his head into that dreadful hole,
And as he slowly drew up, snake-easing his shoulders,
        and entered farther,
A sort of horror, a sort of protest against his withdrawing into
        that horrid black hole,
Deliberately going into the blackness, and slowly drawing
        himself after,
Overcame me now his back was turned.

I looked round, I put down my pitcher,
I picked up a clumsy log
And threw it at the water-trough with a clatter.

I think it did not hit him,
But suddenly that part of him that was left behind convulsed
        in an undignified haste,
Writhed like lightning, and was gone
Into the black hole, the earth-lipped fissure in the wall-front,
At which, in the intense still noon, I stared with fascination.

And immediately I regretted it.
I thought how paltry, how vulgar, what a mean act!
I despised myself and the voices of my accursed human education.

And I thought of the albatross,
And I wished he would come back, my snake.

For he seemed to me again like a king,
Like a king in exile, uncrowned in the underworld,
Now due to be crowned again.

REPTILES

And so, I missed my chance with one of the lords
Of life.
And I have something to expiate:
A pettiness.

Taormina

BIRDS

"Birds are the life of the skies, and when they fly, they reveal the thoughts of the skies. The eagle flies nearest to the sun, no other bird flies so near. So he brings down the life of the sun, and the power of the sun, in his wings, and men who see him wheeling are filled with the elation of the sun. But all creatures of the sun must dip their mouths in blood, the sun is forever thirsty, thirsting for the brightest exhalation of blood."
"You shall know a bird by his cry, and great birds cry loud, but sing not. The eagle screams when the sun is high, the peacock screams at the dawn, rooks call at evening, when the nightingale sings. And all birds have their voices, each means a different thing."

Turkey-Cock

You ruffled black blossom,
You glossy dark wind.

Your sort of gorgeousness,
Dark and lustrous
And skinny repulsive
And poppy-glossy,
Is the gorgeousness that evokes my most puzzled admiration.

Your aboriginality
Deep, unexplained,
Like a Red Indian darkly unfinished and aloof,
Seems like the black and glossy seeds of countless centuries.

Your wattles are the colour of steel-slag which has been red hot
And is going cold,
Cooling to a powdery, pale-oxidised sky-blue.

Why do you have wattles, and a naked, wattled head?
Why do you arch your naked-set eye with a more-than-comprehensible
      arrogance?

The vulture is bald, so is the condor, obscenely,
But only you have thrown this amazing mantilla of oxidised sky-blue
And hot red over you.

This queer dross shawl of blue and vermilion,
Whereas the peacock has a diadem.

I wonder why.
Perhaps it is a sort of uncanny decoration, a veil of loose skin.

BIRDS

Perhaps it is your assertion, in all this ostentation,
  of raw contradictoriness.
Your wattles drip down like a shawl to your breast
And the point of your mantilla drops across your nose, unpleasantly.

Or perhaps it is something unfinished
A bit of slag still adhering, after your firing in the furnace of creation.

Or perhaps there is something in your wattles of a bull's dew-lap
Which slips down like a pendulum to balance the throbbing mass
  of a generous breast,
The over-drip of a large life hanging in the balance.
Only yours would be a raw, unsmelted life, that will not quite fuse
  into being.

You contract yourself,
You arch yourself as an archer's bow
Which quivers indrawn as you clench your spine
Until your veiled head almost touches backward
To the root-rising of your erected tail.
And one intense and backward-curving frisson
Seizes you as you clench yourself together
Like some fierce magnet bringing its poles together.

Burning, pale positive pole of your wattled head!
And from the darkness of that opposite one
The upstart of your round-barred, sun-round tail!

Whilst between the two, along the tense arch of your back
Blows the magnetic current in fierce blasts,
Ruffling black, shining feathers like lifted mail,
Shuddering storm wind, or a water rushing through.

Your brittle, super-sensual arrogance
Tosses the skinny crape across your brow and down your breast
As you draw yourself upon yourself in insistence.

It is a declaration of such tension in will
As Time has not wished to avouch, nor eternity been able to unbend
Do what it may.
A raw American will, that has never been tempered by life;
You brittle, will-tense bird with a foolish eye.

The peacock lifts his rods of bronze
And struts blue-brilliant out of the far East.
But watch a turkey prancing low on earth
Drumming his vaulted wings, as savages drum
Their rhythms on long-drawn, hollow, sinister drums.
The ponderous, sombre sound of the great drum of Huichilobos
In pyramid Mexico, during sacrifice.
Drum, and the turkey onrush,
Sudden, demonic dauntlessness, full abreast,
All the bronze gloss of all his myriad petals
Each one apart and instant.
Delicate frail crescent of the gentle outline of white
At each feather-tip
So delicate;
Yet the bronze wind-bell suddenly clashing
And the eye over-weening into madness.

Turkey-cock, turkey-cock
Are you the bird of the next dawn?

Has the peacock had his day, does he call in vain, screecher,
        for the sun to rise?
The eagle, the dove, and the barnyard rooster, do they call in vain,
        trying to wake the morrow?

BIRDS

And do you await us, wattled father, Westward?
Will your yell do it?

Take up the trail of the vanished American
Where it disappeared at the foot of the crucifix.
Take up the primordial Indian obstinacy,
The more than human, dense insistence of will,
And disdain, and blankness, and onrush, and prise open the new day
        with them?

The East a dead letter, and Europe moribund. . . . Is that so?
And those sombre, dead, feather-lustrous Aztecs, Amerindians,
In all the sinister splendour of their red blood-sacrifices,
Do they stand under the dawn, half-godly, half-demon,
            awaiting the cry of the turkey-cock?

Or must you go through the fire once more, till you're smelted pure,
Slag-wattled turkey-cock,
Dross-jabot?

Fiesole

Humming-Bird

I can imagine, in some otherworld
Primeval-dumb, far back
In that most awful stillness, that only gasped and hummed,
Humming-birds raced down the avenues.

Before anything had a soul,
While life was a heave of Matter, half inanimate,
This little bit chipped off in brilliance
And went whizzing through the slow, vast, succulent stems.

I believe there were no flowers, then,
In the world where the humming-bird flashed ahead of creation.
I believe he pierced the slow vegetable veins with his long beak.

Probably he was big
As mosses and little lizards, they say were once big.
Probably he was a jabbing, terrifying monster.

We look at him through the wrong end of the long telescope of Time,
Luckily for us.

Española

Eagle in New Mexico

Toward the sun, towards the south-west
A scorched breast.
A scorched breast, breasting the sun like an answer,
Like a retort.

An eagle at the top of a low cedar-bush
On the sage-ash desert
Reflecting the scorch of the sun from his breast;
Eagle, with the sickle dripping darkly above.

Erect, scorched-pallid out of the hair of the cedar,
Erect, with the god-thrust entering him from below,
Eagle gloved in feathers
In scorched white feathers
In burnt dark feathers
In feathers still fire-rusted;
Sickle-overswept, sickle dripping over and above.

Sun-breaster,
Staring two ways at once, to right and left;
Masked-one
Dark-visaged
Sickle-masked
With iron between your two eyes;
You feather-gloved
To the feet;
Foot-fierce;
Erect one;
The god-thrusting entering you steadily from below.

You never look at the sun with your two eyes.
Only the inner eye of your scorched broad breast
Looks straight at the sun.

You are dark
Except scorch-pale breasted;
And dark cleaves down and weapon-hard downward curving
At your scorched breast,
Like a sword of Damocles,
Beaked eagle.

You've dipped it in blood so many times
That dark face-weapon, to temper it well,
Blood-thirsty bird.

Why do you front the sun so obstinately,
American eagle?
As if you owed him an old, old grudge, great sun: or an old,
        old allegiance.

When you pick the red smoky heart from a rabbit or
        a light-blooded bird
Do you lift it to the sun, as the Aztec priests used to lift red hearts
        of men?

Does the sun need stream of blood do you think
In America, still,
Old eagle?

Does the sun in New Mexico sail like a fiery bird of prey in the sky
Hovering?
Does he shriek for blood?
Does he fan great wings above the prairie, like a hovering,
        blood-thirsty bird?

BIRDS

And are you his priest, big eagle
Whom the Indians aspire to?
Is there a bond of bloodshed between you?

Is your continent cold from the ice-age still, that the sun is so angry?
Is the blood of your continent somewhat reptilian still,
That the sun should be greedy for it?

I don't yield to you, big, jowl-faced eagle.
Nor you nor your blood-thirsty sun
That sucks up blood
Leaving a nervous people.

Fly off, big bird with a big black back,
Fly slowly away, with a rust of fire in your tail,
Dark as you are on your dark side, eagle of heaven.

Even the sun in heaven can be curbed and chastened at last
By the life in the hearts of men.
And you, great bird, sun-starer, your heavy black beak
Can be put out of office as sacrifice bringer.

Taos

The Blue Jay

The blue jay with a crest on his head
Comes round the cabin in the snow.
He runs in the snow like a bit of blue metal,
Turning his back on everything.

From the pine-tree that towers like a pillar of shaggy smoke
Immense above the cabin
Comes a strident laugh as we approach, this little black dog and I.
So halts the little black bitch on four spread paws in the snow
And looks up inquiringly into the pillar of cloud,
With a tinge of misgiving.
Ca-a-a! comes the scrape of ridicule out of the tree.

What voice of the Lord is that, from the tree of smoke?

Oh Bibbles, little black bitch in the snow,
With a pinch of snow in the groove of your silly snub nose,
What do you look at *me* for?
What do you look at me for, with such misgiving?

It's the blue jay laughing at us.
It's the blue jay jeering at us, Bibs.

Every day since the snow is here
The blue jay paces round the cabin, very busy, picking up bits,
Turning his back on us all,
And bobbing his thick dark crest about the snow, as if darkly saying:
I ignore those folk who look out.

You acid-blue metallic bird,
You thick bird with a strong crest

BIRDS

Who are you?
Whose boss are you, with all your bully way?
You copper-sulphate blue bird!

Lobo

ANIMALS

"Yes, and if oxen or lions had hands, and could paint with their hands, and produce works of art as men do, horses would paint the forms of the gods like horses, and oxen like oxen, and make their bodies in the image of their several kinds."

"Once, they say, he was passing by when a dog was being beaten, and he spoke this word: 'Stop! don't beat it! For it is the soul of a friend I recognised when I heard its voice.'"

"Swine wash in mire, and barnyard fowls in dust."

The Ass

The long-drawn bray of the ass
In the Sicilian twilight—

All mares are dead!
All mares are dead!
Oh-h!
Oh-h-h-h!
Oh-h-h-h—h!!
I can't bear it, I can't bear it,
I can't!
Oh, I can't!
Oh—
There's one left!
There's one left!
One!
There's one ... left. ...

So ending on a grunt of agonised relief.

This is the authentic Arabic interpretation of the braying of the ass.
And Arabs should know.

And yet, as his brass-resonant howling yell resounds through
        the Sicilian twilight
I am not sure—

His big, furry head,
His big, regretful eyes,
His diminished, drooping hindquarters,
His small toes.

ANIMALS

Such a dear!
Such an ass!
With such a knot inside him!
He regrets something that he remembers.
That's obvious.

The Steppes of Tartary,
And the wind in his teeth for a bit,
And *noli me tangere*

Ah then, when he tore the wind with his teeth,
And trod wolves underfoot,
And over-rode his mares as if he were savagely leaping an obstacle,
    to set his teeth in the sun. . . .

Somehow, alas, he fell in love,
And was sold into slavery.

He fell into the rut of love,
Poor ass, like man, always in rut,
The pair of them alike in that.

All his soul in his gallant member
And his head gone heavy with the knowledge of desire
And humiliation.

The ass was the first of all animals to fall finally into love,
From obstacle-leaping pride,
Mare obstacle,
Into love, mare-goal, and the knowledge of love.

Hence Jesus rode him in the Triumphant Entry.
Hence his beautiful eyes.

Hence his ponderous head, brooding over desire, and downfall, Jesus,
　　and a pack-saddle,
Hence he uncovers his big ass-teeth and howls in that agony that
　　half is insatiable desire and half unquenchable humiliation.
Hence the black cross on his shoulders.

The Arabs were only half right, though they hinted the whole:
Everlasting lament in everlasting desire.

See him standing with his head down, near the Porta Cappucini.
Asinello,
Somaro;
With the half-veiled, beautiful eyes, and the pensive face not asleep,
Motionless, like a bit of rock.

Has he seen the Gorgon's head, and turned to stone?
Alas, Love did it.
Now he's a jackass, a pack-ass, a donkey, somaro, burro, with a boss
　　piling loads on his back.
Tied by the nose at the Porta Cappucini
And tied in a knot, inside, deadlocked between two desires:
To overleap like a male all mares as obstacles
In a leap at the sun;
And to leap in one last heart-bursting leap like a male at the goal
　　of a mare,
And there end.

Well, you can't have it both roads.

Hee! Hee! Ehee! Ehaw! Ehaw!! Oh! Oh! Oh-h-h!!
The wave of agony bursts in the stone that he was,
Bares his long ass's teeth, flattens his long ass's ears, straightens
　　his donkey neck,
And howls his pandemonium on the indignant air.

ANIMALS

Yes, it's a quandary.
Jesus rode on him, the first burden on the first beast of burden.
Love on a submissive ass.
So the tale began.

But the ass never forgets.

The horse, being nothing but a nag, will forget.
The men, being mostly geldings and knacker-boned hacks,
      have almost all forgot.
But the ass is a primal creature, and never forgets.

The Steppes of Tartary,
And Jesus on a meek ass-colt: mares: Mary escaping to Egypt:
      Joseph's cudgel.

Hee! Hee! Ehee! Ehow-ow!-ow!-aw!-aw!-aw!
All mares are dead!
Or else I am dead!
One of us, or the pair of us,
I don't know-ow!-ow!
Which!
Not sure-ure-ure
Quite which!
Which!

Taormina

He-Goat

See his black nose snubbed back, pressed over like
    a whale's blow-holes,
As if his nostrils were going to curve back to the root of his tail.

As he charges slow among the herd
And rows among the females like a ship pertinaciously,
Heavy with a rancid cargo, through the lesser ships—
Old father
Sniffing forever ahead of him, at the rear of the goats, that they lift
    the little door,
And rowing on, unarrived, no matter how often he enter:
Like a big ship pushing her bow-sprit over the little ships
Then swerving and steering afresh
And never, never arriving at journey's end, at the rear
    of the female ships.

Yellow eyes incomprehensible with thin slits
To round-eyed us.

Yet if you had whorled horns of bronze in a frontal dark wall
At the end of a back-bone ridge, like a straight sierra roqueña,
And nerves urging forward to the wall, you'd have eyes like his,
Especially if, being given a needle's eye of egress elsewhere
You tried to look back to it, and couldn't.

Sometimes he turns with a start, to fight, to challenge, to suddenly
butt.
And then you see the God that he is, in a cloud of black hair
And storm-lightning-slitted eye.
Splendidly planting his feet, one rocky foot striking the ground with
    a sudden rock-hammer announcement:

ANIMALS

I am here!

And suddenly lowering his head, the whorls of bone and of horn
Slowly revolving towards unexploded explosion,
As from the stem of his bristling, lightning-conductor tail
In a rush up the shrieking duct of his vertebral way
Runs a rage drawn in from the ether divinely through him
Towards a shock and a crash and a smiting of horns ahead.

That is a grand old lust of his, to gather the great
Rage of the sullen-stagnating atmosphere of goats
And bring it hurtling to a head, with crash of horns against the horns
Of the opposite enemy goat,
Thus hammering the mettle of goats into proof, and smiting out
The godhead of goats from the shock.
Things of iron are beaten on the anvil,
And he-goat is anvil to he-goat, and hammer to he-goat
In the business of beating the mettle of goats to a godhead.

But they've taken his enemy from him
And left him only his libidinousness,
His nostrils turning back, to sniff at even himself
And his slitted eyes seeking the needle's eye,
His own, unthreaded, forever.

So it is, when they take the enemy from us,
And we can't fight.

He is not fatherly, like the bull, massive Providence of hot blood;
The goat is an egoist, aware of himself, devilish aware of himself,
And full of malice prepense, and overweening, determined to stand
      on the highest peak
Like the devil, and look on the world as his own.

And as for love:
With a needle of long red flint he stabs in the dark

At the living rock he is up against;
While she with her goaty mouth stands smiling the while as he strikes,
     since sure
He will never *quite* strike home, on the target-quick, for her quick
Is just beyond the range of the arrow he shoots
From his leap at the zenith in her, so it falls just short of the mark,
     far enough.
It is over before it is finished.
She, smiling with goaty munch-mouth, Mona Lisa, arranges it so.

Orgasm after orgasm after orgasm
And he smells so rank, and his nose goes back,
And never an enemy brow-metalled to thresh it out with
     in the open field;
Never a mountain peak, to be king of the castle.
Only those eternal females to overleap and surpass, and never succeed.

The involved voluptuousness of the soft-footed cat
Who is like a fur folding a fur,
The cat who laps blood, and knows
The soft welling of blood invincible even beyond bone or metal of bone.

The soft, the secret, the unfathomable blood
The cat has lapped
And known it subtler than frisson-shaken nerves,
Stronger than multiplicity of bone on bone
And darker than even the arrows of violentest will
Can pierce, for that is where will gives out, like a sinking stone
     that can sink no further.

But he-goat,
Black procreant male of the egoistic will and libidinous desire,
God in black cloud with curving horns of bronze,
Find an enemy, egoist, and clash the cymbals in face-to-face defiance,
And let the lightning out of your smothered dusk.

A N I M A L S

Forget the female herd for a bit,
And fight for your egoist's will;
Fight, old Satan with a selfish will, fight for your selfish will;
Fight to be the devil on the tip of the peak
Overlooking the world for his own.

But bah, how can he, poor domesticated beast!

Taormina

She-Goat

Goats go past the back of the house like dry leaves in the dawn,
And up the hill like a river, if you watch.

At dusk they patter back like a bough being dragged on the ground,
Raising dust and acridity of goats, and bleating.

Our old goat we tie up at night in the shed at the back of the broken
      Greek tomb in the garden,
And when the herd goes by at dawn she begins to bleat for me
      to come down and untie her.

Merr-err-err! Merr-er-errr! Mer! Mé!
Wait, wait a bit, I'll come when I've lit the fire.
Merrr!
Exactly.
Mé! Mer! Merrrrrrr!!!
Tace, tu, crapa, bestia!
Merr-ererrr-ererrrr! Merrrr!

She is such an alert listener, with her ears wide, to know am I coming!
Such a canny listener, from a distance, looking upwards, lending first
      one ear, then another.

There she is, perched on her manger, looking over the boards
      into the day
Like a belle at her window.
And immediately she sees me she blinks, stares, doesn't know me,
      turns her head and ignores me vulgarly with a wooden blank
      on her face.

What do I care for her, the ugly female, standing up there
      with her long tangled sides like old rugs thrown over a fence.

ANIMALS

But she puts her nose down shrewdly enough when the knot is
untied,
And jumps staccato to earth, a sharp, dry jump, still ignoring me,
Pretending to look round the stall.

Come on, you crapa! I'm not your servant!

She turns her head away with an obtuse, female sort of deafness, bête.
And then invariably she crouches her rear and makes water.
That being her way of answer, if I speak to her—self-conscious!
Le bestie non parlano, poverine!

She was bought at Giardini fair, on the sands, for six hundred lire.

An obstinate old witch, almost jerking the rope from my hands
            to eat the acanthus, or bite at the almond buds,
            and make me wait.
Yet the moment I hate her she trips mild and smug like a woman
            going to mass.
The moment I really detest her.

Queer it is, suddenly, in the garden
To catch sight of her standing like some huge, ghoulish grey bird
            in the air, on the bough of the leaning almond tree,
Straight as a board on the bough, looking down like some hairy horrid
            God the Father in a William Blake imagination.
Come down, crapa, out of that almond tree!

Instead of which she strangely rears on her perch in the air, vast beast,
And strangely paws the air, delicate,
And reaches her black-striped face up like a snake, far up,
Subtly, to the twigs overhead, far up, vast beast,
And snaps them sharp, with a little twist of her anaconda head;
All her great hairy shaggy belly open against the morning.

At seasons she curls back her tail like a green leaf in the fire,
Or like a lifted hand, hailing at her wrong end.
And having exposed the pink place of her nakedness, fixedly,
She trots on blithe toes,
And if you look at her, she looks back with a cold, sardonic stare.
Sardonic, sardonyx, rock of cold fire.
See me? she says, *That's me!*

That's her.

Then she leaps the rocks like a quick rock,
Her back-bone sharp as a rock,
Sheer will.
Along which ridge of libidinous magnetism
Defiant, curling the leaf of her tail as if she were curling her lip
> behind her at all life,
Libidinous desire runs back and forth, asserting itself in that little
> lifted bare hand.

Yet she has such adorable spurty kids, like spurts of black ink.
And in a month again is as if she had never had them.

And when the billy goat mounts her
She is brittle as brimstone.
While his slitted eyes squint back to the roots of his ears.

Taormina

Elephant

You go down shade to the river, where naked men sit on flat brown
    rocks, to watch the ferry, in the sun;
And you cross the ferry with the naked people, go up the tropical lane
Through the palm-trees and past hollow paddy-fields where naked men
    are threshing rice
And the monolithic water-buffaloes, like old, muddy stones
    with hair on them, are being idle;
And through the shadow of bread-fruit trees, with their dark green,
    glossy, fanged leaves
Very handsome, and some pure yellow fanged leaves;
Out into the open, where the path runs on the top of a dyke
    between paddy-fields:
And there, of course, you meet a huge and mud-grey elephant
    advancing his frontal bone, his trunk curled round a log of wood:
So you step down the bank, to make way.

Shuffle, shuffle, and his little wicked eye has seen you as he advances
    above you,
The slow beast curiously spreading his round feet for the dust.
And the slim naked man slips down, and the beast deposits
    the lump of wood, carefully.
The keeper hooks the vast knee, the creature salaams.

White man, you are saluted.
Pay a few cents.

But the best is the Pera-hera, at midnight, under the tropical stars,
With a pale little wisp of a Prince of Wales, diffident, up in a small
    pagoda on the temple side
And white people in evening dress buzzing and crowding the stand
    upon the grass below and opposite:

And at last the Pera-hera procession, flambeaux aloft in the tropical
     night, of blazing cocoanut,
Naked dark men beneath,
And the huge frontal of three great elephants stepping forth
     to the tom-tom's beat, in the torch-light,
Slowly sailing in gorgeous apparel through the flame-light, in front of
     a towering, grimacing white image of wood.

The elephant bells striking slow, tong-tong, tong-tong,
To music and queer chanting:
Enormous shadow-processions filing on in the flare of fire
In the fume of cocoa-nut oil, in the sweating tropical night,
In the noise of the tom-toms and singers;
Elephants after elephants curl their trunks, vast shadows,
     and some cry out
As they approach and salaam, under the dripping fire of the torches
That pale fragment of a Prince up there, whose motto is *Ich dien.*

Pale, dispirited Prince, with his chin on his hands, his nerves tired out,
Watching and hardly seeing the trunk-curl approach and clumsy,
     knee-lifting salaam
Of the hugest, oldest of beasts, in the night and the fire-flare below.

He is white men's royalty, pale and dejected fragment up aloft.
And down below huge homage of shadowy beasts bare-foot and
     trunk-lipped in the night.

Chieftains, three of them abreast, on foot
Strut like peg-tops, wound around with hundreds of yards of fine linen.
They glimmer with tissue of gold, and golden threads on
     a jacket of velvet,
And their faces are dark, and fat, and important.

A N I M A L S

They are different royalty, dark-faced royalty, showing the conscious
      whites of their eyes
And stepping in homage, stubborn, to that nervous pale lad up there.

More elephants, tong, tong-tong, loom up,
Huge, more tassels swinging, more dripping fire of new
      cocoa-nut cressets
High, high flambeaux, smoking of the east;
And scarlet hot embers of torches knocked out of the sockets
      among bare feet of elephants and men on the path in the dark.
And devil dancers, luminous with sweat, dancing on to the shudder
      of drums,
Tom-toms, weird music of the devil, voices of men from the
      jungle singing;
Endless, under the Prince.

Towards the tail of the everlasting procession
In the long hot night, mere dancers from insignificant villages,
And smaller, more frightened elephants.

Men-peasants from jungle villages dancing and running with sweat
      and laughing,
Naked dark men with ornaments on, on their naked arms
      and their naked breasts, the grooved loins
Gleaming like metal with running sweat as they suddenly turn,
      feet apart,
And dance and dance, forever dance, with breath half sobbing
      in dark, sweat-shining breasts,
And lustrous great tropical eyes unveiled now, gleaming
      a kind of laugh,
A naked, gleaming dark laugh, like a secret out in the dark,
And flare of a tropical energy, tireless, afire in the dark, slim limbs
      and breasts,
Perpetual, fire-laughing motion, among the slow shuffle
Of elephants,

The hot dark blood of itself a-laughing, wet, half-devilish,
    men all motion
Approaching under that small pavilion, and tropical eyes dilated
    turn up
Inevitably looking up
To the Prince
To that tired remnant of white royalty up there
Whose motto is *Ich dien.*

As if the homage of the kindled blood of the east
Went up in wavelets to him, from the breasts and eyes of
    jungle torch-men,
And he couldn't take it.

What would they do, those jungle men running with sweat,
    with the strange dark laugh in their eyes, glancing up,
And the sparse-haired elephants slowly following,
If they knew that his motto was *Ich dien?*
And that he meant it.

They begin to understand,
The rickshaw boys begin to understand;
And then the devil comes into their faces,
But a different sort, a cold, rebellious, jeering devil.

In elephants and the east are two devils, in all men maybe.
The mystery of the dark mountain of blood, reeking in homage,
    in lust, in rage,
And passive with everlasting patience,
Then the little, cunning pig-devil of the elephant's lurking eyes,
    the unbeliever.

We dodged, when the Pera-hera was finished, under the hanging,
    hairy pig's tails

ANIMALS

And the flat, flaccid mountains of the elephants' standing haunches,
Vast-blooded beasts,
Myself so little dodging rather scared against the eternal wrinkled
     pillars of their legs, as they were being dismantled;
Then I knew they were dejected, having come to hear the repeated
Royal summons: *Dient Ihr!*
Serve!
Serve, vast mountainous blood, in submission and splendour,
     serve royalty.
Instead of which, the silent, fatal emission from that nervous pale boy
     up there:
Ich dien.

That's why the night fell in frustration.
That's why, as the elephants ponderously, with unseeming swiftness
     galloped uphill in the night, going back to the jungle villages,
As the elephant bells sounded tong-tong-tong, bell of the temple
     of blood, in the night, swift-striking,
And the crowd like a field of rice in the dark gave way like liquid
     to the dark
Looming gallop of the beasts,
It was as if the great bare bulks of elephants in the festive night went
     over the hill-brow swiftly, with their tails between their legs,
     in haste to get away,
Their bells sounding frustrate and sinister.

And all the dark-faced, cotton-wrapped people, more numerous and
     whispering than grains of rice in a rice-field at night,
All the dark-faced, cotton-wrapped people, a countless host on the
     shores of the lake, with thick wild rice by the water's edge,
Waiting for the fireworks of the after-show,
As the rockets went up, and the glare passed over countless faces,
     dark as black rice growing,
Showing a glint of teeth, and glancing tropical eyes aroused
     in the night,

There was the faintest twist of mockery in every face, across the hiss
    of wonders as the rocket burst
High, high up, in flakes, shimmering flakes of blue fire, above the
    palm trees of the islet in the lake.
Oh faces upturned to the glare, oh tropical wonder, wonder,
    a miracle in heaven!
And the shadow of a jeer, of underneath disappointment, as the
    rocket-coruscation died, and shadow was the same as before.

They were foiled, the myriad whispering dark-faced
    cotton-wrapped people.
They had come to see royalty,
To bow before royalty, in the land of elephants, bow deep, bow deep.
Bow deep, for it's good as a draught of cool water to bow
    very, very low to the royal.

And all there was to bow to, an alien, diffident boy whose motto is
    Ich dien.
I serve! I serve! in all the weary irony of his mien—*'Tis I who serve!*
Drudge to the public.

I wish some dark-faced man could have taken the feathers three
And fearless gone up the pavilion, in that pepper-box aloft and alone
Held the three feathers out on the night, with a dark, fierce hand
    above the host,
Saying softly: *Dient Ihr! Dient!*
Omnes, vos omnes, servite.
Serve me, I am meet to be served.
Being royal of the gods.

I with the feathers.
I with the flower-de-luce.
I with the scarab-wings.
I from the marshes of blood,
Am back again.

ANIMALS

And to the elephants:
First great beasts of the earth
A prince has come back to you,
Blood-mountains.
Crook the knee and be glad.

Kandy

Kangaroo

In the northern hemisphere
Life seems to leap at the air, or skim under the wind
Like stags on rocky ground, or pawing horses, or springy
     scut-tailed rabbits.

Or else rush horizontal to charge at the sky's horizon,
Like bulls or bisons or wild pigs.

Or slip like water slippery towards its ends,
As foxes, stoats, and wolves, and prairie dogs.

Only mice, and moles, and rats, and badgers, and beavers,
     and perhaps bears
Seem belly-plumbed to the earth's mid-navel.
Or frogs that when they leap come flop, and flop to the centre
     of the earth.

But the yellow antipodal Kangaroo, when she sits up,
Who can unseat her, like a liquid drop that is heavy,
     and just touches earth.

The downward drip.
The down-urge.
So much denser than cold-blooded frogs.

Delicate mother Kangaroo
Sitting up there rabbit-wise, but huge, plumb-weighted,
And lifting her beautiful slender face, oh! so much more gently
     and finely-lined than a rabbit's, or than a hare's,
Lifting her face to nibble at a round white peppermint drop,
     which she loves, sensitive mother Kangaroo.

ANIMALS

Her sensitive, long, pure-bred face.
Her full antipodal eyes, so dark,
So big and quiet and remote, having watched so many empty dawns
    in silent Australia.

Her little loose hands, and drooping Victorian shoulders.
And then her great weight below the waist, her vast pale belly
With a thin young yellow little paw hanging out, and straggle of
    a long thin ear, like ribbon,
Like a funny trimming to the middle of her belly, thin little dangle
    of an immature paw, and one thin ear.

Her belly, her big haunches
And in addition, the great muscular python-stretch of her tail.

There, she shan't have any more peppermint drops.
So she wistfully, sensitively sniffs the air, and then turns, goes off
    in slow sad leaps
On the long flat skis of her legs,
Steered and propelled by that steel-strong snake of a tail.

Stops again, half turns, inquisitive to look back.
While something stirs quickly in her belly, and a lean little face
    comes out, as from a window,
Peaked and a bit dismayed,
Only to disappear again quickly away from the sight of the world,
    to snuggle down in the warmth,
Leaving the trail of a different paw hanging out.

Still she watches with eternal, cocked wistfulness!
How full her eyes are, like the full, fathomless, shining eyes
    of an Australian black-boy
Who has been lost so many centuries on the margins of existence!

She watches with insatiable wistfulness.
Untold centuries of watching for something to come,
For a new signal from life, in that silent lost land of the South.

Where nothing bites but insects and snakes and the sun, small life.
Where no bull roared, no cow ever lowed, no stag cried,
      no leopard screeched, no lion coughed, no dog barked,
But all was silent save for parrots occasionally, in the haunted
      blue bush.

Wistfully watching, with wonderful liquid eyes.
And all her weight, all her blood, dripping sack-wise down towards
      the earth's centre,
And the live little one taking in its paw at the door of her belly.

Leap then, and come down on the line that draws to the earth's deep,
      heavy centre.

Sydney

Bibbles

Bibbles
Little black dog in New Mexico,
Little black snub-nosed bitch with a shoved-out jaw
And a wrinkled reproachful look;
Little black female pup, sort of French bull, they say,
With bits of brindle coming through, like rust, to show
        you're not pure;
Not pure, Bibbles,
Bubsey, bat-eared dog;
Not black enough!

First live thing I've "owned" since the lop-eared rabbits
        when I was a lad,
And those over-prolific white mice, and Adolf, and Rex
        whom I didn't own.
And even now, Bibbles, little Ma'am, it's you who appropriated me,
        not I you.
As Benjamin Franklin appropriating Providence to his purposes.

Oh Bibbles, black little bitch
I'd never have let you appropriate me, had I known.
I never dreamed, till now, of the awful time the Lord must have,
        "owning" humanity,
Especially democratic live-by-love humanity.

Oh Bibbles, oh Pips, oh Pipsey
You little black love-bird!
Don't you love *everybody!!!*
Just everybody.
You love 'em all.
Believe in the One Identity, don't you,
You little Walt-Whitmanesque bitch?

First time I lost you in Taos plaza,
And found you after endless chasing,
Came upon you prancing round the corner in exuberant,
     bibbling affection
After the black-green skirts of a yellow-green old Mexican woman
Who hated you, and kept looking round at you and cursing you
     in a mutter,
While you pranced and bounced with love of her,
     you indiscriminating animal,
All your wrinkled *miserere* Chinese black little face beaming
And your black little body bouncing and wriggling
With indiscriminate love, Bibbles;
I had a moment's pure detestation of you.

As I rushed like an idiot round the corner after you
Yelling: *Pips! Pips! Bibbles!*

I've had moments of hatred of you since,
Loving everybody!
"To you, whoever you are, with endless embrace!"—
That's you, Pipsey,
With your imbecile bit of a tail in a love-flutter.
You omnipip.

Not that you're merely a softy, oh dear me no,
You know which side your bread is buttered.
You don't care a rap for anybody.
But you love lying warm between warm human thighs, indiscriminate,
You love to make somebody love you, indiscriminate,
You love to lap up affection, to wallow in it,
And then turn tail to the next comer, for a new dollop.

And start prancing and licking and cuddling again, indiscriminate.

Oh yes, I know your little game.

ANIMALS

Yet you're so nice,
So quick, like a little black dragon.
So fierce, when the coyotes howl, barking back like a whole little lion,
    and rumbling,
And starting forward in the dusk, with your little black fur all bristling
    like plush
Against those coyotes, who would swallow you like an oyster.

And in the morning, when the bedroom door is opened,
Rushing in like a little black whirlwind, leaping straight as an arrow
    on the bed at the pillow
And turning the day suddenly into a black tornado of *joie de vivre*,
    Chinese dragon.

So funny
Lobbing wildly through deep snow like a rabbit,
Hurtling like a black ball through the snow,
Champing it, tossing a mouthful,
Little black spot in the landscape!

So absurd
Pelting behind on the dusty trail when the horse sets off home
    at a gallop:
Left in the dust behind like a dust-ball tearing along
Coming up on fierce little legs, tearing fast to catch up, a real little
    dust-pig, ears almost blown away,
And black eyes bulging bright in a dust-mask
Chinese-dragon-wrinkled, with a pink mouth grinning under jaw
    shoved out
And white teeth showing in your dragon-grin as you race,
    you split-face,
Like a trundling projectile swiftly whirling up,
Cocking your eyes at me as you come alongside, to see if
    I'm on the horse,

And panting with that split grin,
All your game little body dust-smooth like a little pig, poor Pips.

Plenty of game old spirit in you, Bibbles.
Plenty of game old spunk, little bitch.

How you hate being brushed with the boot-brush, to brush
      all that dust out of your wrinkled face,
Don't you?
How you hate being made to look undignified, Ma'am;
How you hate being laughed at, Miss Superb!

Blackberry face!

Plenty of conceit in you.
Unblemished belief in your own perfection
And utter lovableness, you ugly-mug;
Chinese puzzle-face,
Wrinkled underhung physog that looks as if it had finished
      with everything,
Through with everything.

Instead of which you sit there and roll your head like a canary
And show a tiny bunch of white teeth in your underhung blackness,
Self-conscious little bitch,
Aiming again at being loved.

Let the merest scallywag come to the door and you leap
      your very dearest love at him,
As if now, at last, here was the one you *finally* loved,
Finally loved;
And even the dirtiest scallywag is taken in,
Thinking: *This dog sure has taken a fancy to me.*

ANIMALS

You miserable little bitch of love-tricks,
I know your game.

Me or the Mexican who comes to chop wood
All the same,
All humanity is jam to you.

Everybody so dear, and yourself so ultra-beloved
That you have to run out at last and eat filth,
Gobble up filth, you horror, swallow utter abomination,
        and fresh-dropped dung.

You worse than a carrion-crow.
Reeking dung-mouth.
You love-bird.

Reject nothing, sings Walt Whitman.
So you, you go out at last and eat the unmentionable,
In your appetite for affection.

And then you run in to vomit it in my house!
I get my love back.
And I have to clean up after you, filth which even blind Nature rejects
From the pit of your stomach;
But you, you snout-face, you reject nothing, you merge so much in love
You must eat even that.

Then when I skelp you a bit with a juniper twig
You run straight away to live with somebody else,
Fawn before them, and love them as if they were the ones you had
        really loved all along.
And they're taken in.
They feel quite tender over you, till you play the same trick on them,
        dirty bitch.

ANIMALS

Fidelity! Loyalty! Attachment!
Oh, these are abstractions to your nasty little belly.
You must always be a-waggle with LOVE.
Such a waggle of love you can hardly distinguish one human
       from another.

You love one after another, on one condition, that each one
       loves *you* most.
Democratic little bull-bitch, dirt-eating little swine.

But now, my lass, you've got your Nemesis on your track,
Now you've come sex-alive, and the great ranch dogs are all after you.
They're after what they can get, and don't you turn tail!
You loved 'em all so much before, didn't you, loved 'em indiscriminate?
You don't love 'em now.
They want something of you, so you squeak and come pelting indoors.

Come pelting to me, now the other folk have found you out,
       and the dogs are after you.
Oh yes, you're found out. I heard them kick you out of the ranch
house.
Get out, you little, soft fool!!

And didn't you turn your eyes up at me then?
And didn't you cringe on the floor like any inkspot!
And crawl away like a black snail!
And doesn't everybody loathe you then!
And aren't your feelings violated, you high-bred little love-bitch!

For you're sensitive,
In many ways very finely bred.
But bred in conceit that the world is all for love
Of you, my bitch: till you get so far you eat filth.
Fool, in spite of your pretty ways, and quaint, know-all, wrinkled
       old aunty's face.

ANIMALS

So now, what with great Airedale dogs,
And a kick or two,
And a few vomiting bouts,
And a juniper switch,
You look at me for discrimination, don't you?
Look up at me with misgiving in your bulging eyes,
And fear in the smoky whites of your eyes, you nigger;
And you're puzzled,
You think you'd better mind your P's and Q's for a bit,
Your sensitive love-pride being all hurt.

All right, my little bitch.
You learn loyalty rather than loving,
And I'll protect you.

Lobo

Mountain Lion

Climbing through the January snow, into the Lobo canyon
Dark grow the spruce trees, blue is the balsam, water sounds
      still unfrozen, and the trail is still evident.

Men!
Two men!
Men! The only animal in the world to fear!

They hesitate.
We hesitate.
They have a gun.
We have no gun.

Then we all advance, to meet.

Two Mexicans, strangers, emerging out of the dark and snow and
      inwardness of the Lobo valley.
What are they doing here on this vanishing trail?

What is he carrying?
Something yellow.
A deer?

Qué tiene, amigo?
Léon—

He smiles, foolishly, as if he were caught doing wrong.
And we smile, foolishly, as if we didn't know.
He is quite gentle and dark-faced.

A N I M A L S

It is a mountain lion,
A long, slim cat, yellow like a lioness.
Dead.

He trapped her this morning, he says, smiling foolishly.

Lift up her face,
Her round, bright face, bright as frost.
Her round, fine-fashioned head, with two dead ears;
And stripes on the brilliant frost of her face, sharp, fine dark rays,
Dark, keen, fine rays in the brilliant frost of her face.
Beautiful dead eyes.

Hermoso es!

They go out towards the open;
We go on into the gloom of Lobo.

And above the trees I found her lair,
A hole in the blood-orange brilliant rocks that stick up, a little cave.
And bones, and twigs, and a perilous ascent.
So, she will never leap up that way again, with the yellow flash
   of a mountain lion's long shoot!
And her bright striped frost-face will never watch any more,
   out of the shadow of the cave in the blood-orange rock,
Above the trees of the Lobo dark valley-mouth!

Instead, I look out.
And out to the dim of the desert, like a dream, never real;
To the snow of the Sangre de Cristo mountains, the ice of
   the mountains of Picoris,
And near across at the opposite steep of snow, green trees motionless
   standing in snow, like a Christmas toy.

And I think in this empty world there was room for me
    and a mountain lion.
And I think in the world beyond, how easily we might spare a million
    or two of humans
And never miss them.
Yet what a gap in the world, the missing white frost-face of that slim
    yellow mountain lion!

Lobo

The Red Wolf

Over the heart of the west, the Taos desert
Circles an eagle,
And it's dark between me and him.

The sun, as he waits a moment, huge and liquid
Standing without feet on the rim of the far-off mesa
Says: *Look for a last long time then! Look! Look well! I am going.*
So he pauses and is beholden, and straightway is gone.

And the Indian, in a white sheet
Wrapped to the eyes, the sheet bound close on his brows,
Stands saying: *See, I'm invisible!*
Behold how you can't behold me!
The invisible in its shroud!

Now that the sun has gone, and the aspen leaves
And the cotton-wood leaves are fallen, as good as fallen,
And the ponies are in corral,
And it's night:

Why, more has gone than all these;
And something has come.
A red wolf stands on the shadow's dark red rim.

Day has gone to dust on the sage-grey desert
Like a white Christus fallen to dust from a cross;
To dust, to ash, on the twilit floor of the desert.
And a black crucifix like a dead tree spreading wings;
Maybe a black eagle with its wings out
Left lonely in the night
In a sort of worship.

And coming down upon us, out of the dark concave
Of the eagle's wings,
And the coffin-like slit where the Indian's eyes are,
And the absence of cotton-wood leaves, or of aspen,
Even the absence of dark-crossed donkeys:
Come tall old demons, smiling
The Indian smile,
Saying: *How do you do, you pale-face?*

I am very well, old demon.
How are you?

Call me Harry if you will,
Call me Old Harry, says he.
Or the abbreviation of Nicolas,
Nick, Old Nick, maybe.

Well, you're a dark old demon,
And I'm a pale-face like a homeless dog
That has followed the sun from the dawn through the east
Trotting east and east and east till the sun himself went home,
And left me homeless here in the dark at your door.
How do you think we'll get on,
Old demon, you and I?

You and I, you pale-face
Pale-face you and I
Don't get on.

Mightn't we try?

Where's your God, you white one?
Where's your white God?

ANIMALS

He fell to dust as the twilight fell,
Was fume as I trod
The last step out of the east.

Then you're a lost white dog of a pale-face,
And the day's now dead. . . .

Touch me carefully, old father,
My beard is red.

Thin red wolf of a pale-face,
Thin red wolf, go home.

I have no home, old father.
That's why I come.

We take no hungry stray from the pale-face . . .

Father, you are not asked.
I am come. I am here. The red-dawn-wolf
Sniffs round your place.
Lifts up his voice and howls to the walls of the pueblo
Announcing he's here.

The dogs of the dark pueblo
Have long fangs . . .

Has the red wolf trotted east and east and east,
From the far, far other end of the day
To fear a few fangs?

Across the pueblo river
That dark old demon and I
Thus say a few words to each other

And wolf, he calls me, and red.
I call him no names.
He says, however, he is Star-Road.
I say, he can go back the same gait.

As for me . . .
Since I trotted at the tail of the sun as far as ever the creature
          went east,
And lost him here,
I'm going to sit down on my tail right here
And wait for him to come back with a new story.
I'm the red wolf, says the dark old father.
All right, the red dawn wolf I am.

Taos

GHOSTS

And as "the dog with its nostrils tracking out the fragments of the beasts' limbs, and the breath from their feet that they leave in the soft grass," runs upon a path that is pathless to men, so does the soul follow the trail of the dead, across great spaces. For the journey is a far one, to sleep and a forgetting, and often the dead look back, and linger, for now they realise all that is lost. Then the living soul comes up with them, and great is the pain of greeting, and deadly the parting again. For oh, the dead are disconsolate, since even death can never make up for some mistakes.

Men in New Mexico

Mountains blanket-wrapped
Round a white hearth of desert—

While the sun goes round
And round and round the desert,
The mountains never get up and walk about.
They can't, they can't wake.

They camped and went to sleep
In the last twilight
Of Indian gods;
And they can't wake.

Indians dance and run and stamp—
No good.
White men make gold-mines and the mountains unmake them
In their sleep.

The Indians laugh in their sleep
From fear,
Like a man when he sleeps and his sleep is over, and he can't wake up,
And he lies like a log and screams and his scream is silent
Because his body can't wake up;
So he laughs from fear, pure fear, in the grip of the sleep.

A dark membrane over the will holding a man down
Even when the mind has flickered awake;
A membrane of sleep, like a black blanket.

We walk in our sleep, in this land,
Somnambulist wide-eyed afraid.

GHOSTS

We scream for someone to wake us
And our scream is soundless in the paralysis of sleep,
And we know it.

The Penitentes lash themselves till they run with blood
In their efforts to come awake for one moment;
To tear the membrane of this sleep . . .
No good.

The Indians thought the white man would awake them . . .
And instead, the white men scramble asleep in the mountains,
And ride on horseback asleep forever through the desert,
And shoot one another, amazed and mad with somnambulism,
Thinking death will awaken something . . .
No good.

Born with a caul,
A black membrane over the face,
And unable to tear it
Though the mind is awake.

Mountains blanket-wrapped
Round the ash-white hearth of the desert;
And though the sun leaps like a thing unleashed in the sky
They can't get up, they are under the blanket.

Taos

Autumn at Taos

Over the rounded sides of the Rockies, the aspens of autumn,
The aspens of autumn,
Like yellow hair of a tigress brindled with pine.

Down on my hearth-rug of desert, sage of the mesa,
An ash-grey pelt
Of wolf all hairy and level, a wolf's wild pelt.

Trot-trot to the mottled foot-hills, cedar-mottled and piñon:
Did you ever see an otter?
Silver-sided, fish-fanged, fierce-faced, whiskered, mottled.

When I trot my little pony through the aspen trees of the canyon,
Behold me trotting at east betwixt the slopes of the golden
Great and glistening-feathered legs of the hawk of Horus;
The golden hawk of Horus
Astride above me.

But under the pines
I go slowly
As under the hairy belly of a great black bear.

Glad to emerge and look back
On the yellow, pointed aspen-trees laid one on another like feathers,
Feather over feather on the breast of the great and golden
Hawk as I say of Horus.

Pleased to be out in the sage and the pine fish-dotted foothills,
Past the otter's whiskers,
On to the fur of the wolf-pelt that strews the plain.

GHOSTS

And then to look back to the rounded sides of the squatting Rockies,
Tigress-brindled with aspen
Jaguar-splashed, puma-yellow, leopard-livid slopes of America.

Make big eyes, little pony
At all these skins of wild beasts;
They won't hurt you.

Fangs and claws and talons and beaks and hawk-eyes
Are nerveless just now.
So be easy.

Taos

Spirits Summoned West

England seems full of graves to me,
Full of graves.

Women I loved and cherished, like my mother;
Yet I had to tell them to die.

England seems covered with graves to me,
Women's graves.

Women who were gentle
And who loved me
And whom I loved
And told to die.

Women with the beautiful eyes of the old days,
Belief in love, and sorrow of such belief.
"Hush, my love, then, hush.
Hush, and die, my dear!"

Women of the older generation, who knew
The full doom of loving and not being able to take back.
Who understood at last what it was to be told to die.

Now that the graves are made, and covered;
Now that in England pansies and such-like grow on the graves
      of women;
Now that in England is silence, where before was a moving
      of soft-skirted women,
Women with eyes that were gentle in olden belief in love;
Now then that all their yearning is hushed, and covered over
      with earth.

GHOSTS

England seems like one grave to me.

And I, I sit on this high American desert
With dark-wrapped Rocky Mountains motionless squatting around
      in a ring,
Remembering I told them to die, to sink into the grave in England,
The gentle-kneed women.

So now I whisper: *Come away,*
Come away from the place of graves, come west,
Women,
Women whom I loved and told to die.

Come back to me now,
Now the divided yearning is over;
Now you are husbandless indeed, no more husband to cherish
      like a child
And wrestle with for the prize of perfect love.
No more children to launch in a world you mistrust.
Now you need know in part
No longer, nor carry the burden of a man on your heart,
Nor the burden of Man writ large.

Now you are disemburdened of Man and a man
Come back to me.
Now you are free of the toils of a would-be-perfect love
Come to me and be still.

Come back then, you who were wives and mothers
And always virgins
Overlooked.

Come back then, mother, my love, whom I told to die.
It was only I who saw the virgin you
That had no home.

The overlooked virgin,
My love.

You overlooked her too.

Now that the grave is made of mother and wife,
Now that the grave is made and lidded over with turf:

Come, delicate, overlooked virgin, come back to me
And be still,
Be glad.

I didn't tell you to die, for nothing.
I wanted the virgin you to be home at last
In my heart.

Inside my innermost heart,
Where the virgin in woman comes home to a man.

The homeless virgin
Who never in all her life could find the way home
To that difficult innermost place in a man.

Now come west, come home,
Women I've loved for gentleness,
For the virginal you.
Find the way now that you never could find in life,
So I told you to die.
Virginal first and last
Is woman.
Now at this last, my love, my many a love,
You whom I loved for gentleness,
Come home to me.

GHOSTS

There are many, and I loved them, shall always love them,
And they know it,
The virgins.
And my heart is glad to have them at last.

Now that the wife and mother and mistress is buried in earth,
In English earth,
Come home to me, my love, my loves, my many loves,
Come west to me.

For virgins are not exclusive of virgins
As wives are of wives;
And motherhood is jealous,
But in virginity jealousy does not enter.

Taos

THE AMERICAN EAGLE

The Dove of Liberty sat on an egg
And hatched another eagle.

But didn't disown the bird.

Down with all eagles! cooed the Dove.
And down all eagles began to flutter, reeling from their perches:
Eagles with two heads, Eagles with one, presently Eagles with none
Fell from the hooks and were dead.

Till the American Eagle was the only eagle left in the world.

Then it began to fidget, shifting from one leg to the other,
Trying to look like a pelican,
And plucking out of its plumage a few loose feathers to feather
     the nests of all
The new naked little republics come into the world.

But the feathers were, comparatively, a mere flea-bite.
And the bub-eagle that Liberty had hatched was growing
     a startling big bird
On the roof of the world;
A bit awkward, and with a funny squawk in his voice,
His mother Liberty trying always to teach him to coo
And him always ending with a yawp
Coo! Coo! Coo! Coo-ark! Coo-ark!
Quark!! Quark!!

YAWP!!!

So he clears his throat, the young Cock-eagle!

THE AMERICAN EAGLE

Now if the lilies of France lick Solomon in all his glory;
And the leopard cannot change his spots;
Nor the British lion his appetite;
Neither can a young Cock-eagle sit everlastingly
With an olive-sprig in his mouth.

It's not his nature.

The big bird of the Amerindian being the eagle,
Red Men still stick themselves over with bits of his fluff,
And feel absolutely IT.

So better make up your mind, American Eagle,
Whether you're a sucking dove, *Roo—ooo—ooo! Quark! Yawp!!*
Or a pelican
Handing out a few loose golden breast-feathers, at moulting time;
Or a sort of prosperity-fowl
Fathering endless ten-dollar golden eggs.

Or whether it actually is an eagle you are,
With a Roman nose
And claws not made to shake hands with,
And a Me-Almighty eye.

The new full-fledged Republic
Chained to the perch of prosperity.
Overweening bird, full of screams of life, commanding
        a lucrative obedience.
Eagle of the Rockies, bird of men that are greedy,
Flapping your wings from your perch and commanding
        the greedy millions
Burrowing below you.
Opening great wings in the face of the sheep-faced ewe of the world

Who is losing her lamb;
Drinking a little blood, then spitting it out, young eagle, in distaste;
What bird are you, in the end?

What are you, American Eagle?
Will you feed for ever on the cold meat of prosperity?
Was your mother really a pelican, are you a strange cross?
Can you stay forever a tame half-breed cock on a golden perch?
Young eagle? Pelican-boy?

You're such a huge fowl!
And such a puzzler!

Santa Fe

About the Author

DAVID HERBERT LAWRENCE *was born in 1885 in a coal-mining village in the English Midlands. Although best known as a novelist, he was also an important poet. The open form of his mature poetry has had a significant influence on modern and contemporary American poetry. Because he pushed the boundaries of sexual explicitness in his fiction he had to contend with censorship throughout his career.* The Rainbow *(1915) was declared obscene and banned, and* Lady Chatterley's Lover *(1928), his best-known novel, had to be privately printed. From 1920 onwards Lawrence and his German wife Frieda lived in self-exile from England, mostly in Italy, but also in Taos, New Mexico, and Mexico. Lawrence died at the age of 44 in Southern France in 1930.*